THE STREETS OF
BRUM

PART THREE

THE STREETS OF
BRUM
PART THREE

Carl Chinn

BREWIN BOOKS

First published by
Brewin Books Ltd, 56 Alcester Road,
Studley, Warwickshire B80 7LG in 2006
www.brewinbooks.com

ISBN 1 85858 299 7

A Cataloguing in Publication Record
for this title is available from the British Library.

Typeset in Times
Printed in Great Britain by
Cromwell Press.

To
Those Brummies yet unborn to help them
to know who they are

Preface

This is the third volume of a work that I have been researching for as long as I have been studying the history of Birmingham. It is impossible to delve into the city's past without coming into contact with its street names. The city's landscape is shaped by its streets, roads, lanes, alleys and entries as much as it is by its natural physical features such as hills, valleys, streams and rivers; whilst the lives of its people are deeply affected by where they live, work, play and gather socially. Any person, family, group, business, or event that engages the attention of historians is inevitably attached to a street or streets. Without setting out intentionally to discover the origins and histories of Birmingham's streets, I found that I was learning about them through looking at other topics and soon I came to realise how much of our past is encapsulated in the names of our streets. My historical enquiries were enhanced by the fact that as a Brummie I had – like all Brummies – wondered about how streets connected to my family had gained their names.

Originally, I had intended to write one book that included the street and district names of Birmingham. However, I found that I had much too much information for a single work. Accordingly, the district names of Birmingham are covered in *1,000 Years of Brum* (Birmingham: Birmingham Evening Mail, 1999). *The Streets of Brum Part One* followed in 2003 and *The Streets of Brum Part Two* in 2004. Both the previous books and this one can be read separately or as part of a series. In the first volume I focused on a variety of street names beginning with the letters A to E, whilst in the second volume I have attended to streets beginning with the letters F to H. In this volume streets beginning with letters I to M are dealt with. Within each headlined street there is a discussion of closely linked streets that may not begin with these letters. For example, the entry under Inkerman Street also includes explanations about Alma Crescent, Unett Street, Balaclava Road and others – all of which can only be understood in relation to Inkerman Street. Such streets are made bold in the text and are included in the index. Where it is necessary, I have referred to other headline streets that are of relevance to a particular entry. Because of the style of the book there is no list of contents. In effect that is found in the index, whilst the headline streets are gathered in chapters according to the letter of the alphabet to which they pertain. I hope that you find reading this book as fascinating as I have found its research.

I

Icknield Street, Hockley and Brookfields

Since the cutting of the canals and the laying of the railway lines, Birmingham has been at the centre of communications in England. This vital role as a crossing point for the nation has been strengthened by our location at the hub of the modern motorway system. But Birmingham has not always been in such an advantageous spot.

From 1166 it was a growing market and manufacturing town and it did lie across the meeting place of a number of important local routes, but it was a distance away from the great highways such as the Chester Road. Indeed it is from that date that we trace our growth as a significant place. Before then there were plenty of farms and hamlets in and around the manor of Birmingham, but there was no major settlement. That lack of standing was not something that early historians of our town position were prepared to accept. Chief amongst them was William Hutton.

Like so many Brummies, he had been pulled here from elsewhere by the lure of work and of a free society that was not shackled by lords, gilds or bishops. In the preface to his ground-breaking history of Birmingham in 1783, Hutton extolled the

Icknield Street between Hingeston Street and Prescott Street in 1968.

town which had adopted him: 'Birmingham, like a compassionate nurse, not only draws our persons, but our esteem, from the place of our nativity, and fixes it upon herself: I might add, I was hungry, and she fed me; thirsty, and she gave me drink; a stranger, and she took me in. I approached her with reluctance, because I did not know her; I shall leave her with reluctance, because I do.'

The first historian of our city, he enthusiastically melded historical evidence with personal observations and recollections and, at times, wishful thinking. One of his greatest wishes was to claim a prominence for Birmingham in the Roman age. He asserted that the town was 'a place of note in the time of Caesar', basing this bold statement on his belief that an important Roman road called 'Ikenield-Street' had run through Birmingham and that there had been a Roman station called Bremenium close to Warstone Lane.

According to Hutton, Icknield Street was 'one of those famous pretorian roads which marked the Romans with conquest, and the Britons with slavery'. He believed that it began in Southampton and ended at the River Tyne, and that on its way it came through Selly Oak:

> thence by the observatory in Lady Wood-lane, where it enters the parish of Birmingham, crossing the Dudley road at the Sand-pits; along Worstone-lane, through the little pool, and Hockley-brook, where it leaves the parish: thence over Handsworth-heath, entering a little lane on the right of Bristle-lands-end, and over the river Tame, at Offord-house (Oldford) directly to Sutton Coldfield. It passes the Ridgway 126 yards east of King's standing . . . From thence the road proceeds through Sutton-park and the remainder of the Coldfield; over Radley-moor, from thence to Wall, a Roman station . .

Hutton's certainty about the course of the road led to the naming of Icknield Street on the borders of Hockley and Brookfields, although until 1878, when Icknield Street West became Monument Road, it was known as Icknield Street East. Still despite Hutton's determined efforts to make facts of conjecture, there is no evidence for a Roman settlement called Bremenium and because of this generations of later historians have dismissed his other claims as flights of fancy. Yet now, archaeological evidence is affirming that the Romans did have a base within the bounds of modern Birmingham, and that two or more Roman road did run through our city.

The Icknield Street of Hutton gained its name in the Middle Ages and it actually encompasses a number of separate roads. To add to the confusion some people prefer to use the name of Ryknield Street so as not to get mixed up with the more famous Icknield Way. For our purposes, however, Icknield Street came through Alcester, well known for its Roman connections, and headed north to Wall, near to Lichfield.

On its way it came through Beoley and Kings Norton. Some historians state that it then crossed the River Rea at Lifford to follow the modern Lifford Lane and Pershore Road, Stirchley. From there it went via Selly Park and turned so as to go close by Edgbaston Parish Church and thence along what are now Great Hampton Row, Wheeler Street and Wellhead Lane, which originally was in Handsworth. Thence the road crossed the River Tame at Holford, stretching upwards to Kingstanding and Sutton Park, where Hutton was 'struck with astonishment, I thought it the grandest sight I had ever beheld; and was amazed that so noble a monument of antiquity should be so little regarded.'

This road that so impressed Hutton can still be seen in Sutton Park. It is made of gravel and pebble, is 60 foot wide and is flanked by ditches – and it has given its name to Streetly, which means the clearing by the Roman road. This district shares its origin with Stirchley, which originally was Strutley. Other historians argue that Icknield Street took a different route from the Pershore Road, going by way of part of Metchley Lane, Harborne Road, Monument Road and Icknield Street and then crossing the Tame to the west of Holford. This direction is strengthened by the presence of a Roman fort at Metchley.

Hutton himself had been there, explaining that 'in Mitchley Park, three miles west of Birmingham, in the parish of Edgbaston, is *The Camp;* which might be ascribed to the Romans, lying within two or three stones cast of their Ikenield-street'. No part of this fortification was wholly obliterated, 'though in many places it is nearly levelled by modern cultivation—that dreadful enemy to the antiquary', whilst pieces of armour were frequently ploughed up. However, Hutton felt that the camp was made by the Danes and not the Romans. He was wrong.

Given as Mychlehaye in a document from 1350 and meaning the great (micel) enclosure (haeg), Metchley (hence **Metchley Lane** and **Metchley Park Road**) is an exciting place for Brummies, for it pulls us back to the early decades AD. Today its remains lie within the QE Hospital and the main campus and Medical School of the University of Birmingham. Its outline was visible above ground in the early twentieth century and excavations in the 1930s confirmed that it was of a Roman date. These digs were followed by more in the 1940s and 1950s and again since 1997.

Seemingly the fort was built in the early years of the Roman Conquest of Britain, which began in 43 AD, to provide a base as the Roman Army moved north and west. It was defended by a turf and earth bank, a timber wall and towers, and double ditches. Inside were rows of timber buildings, including barrack blocks, a granary, a workshop and a store – all giving room for about 1,000 legionaries.

Later the fort was extended and new buildings were erected, and there is evidence of small-scale industrial activity such as ironworking. Then about 60 AD a smaller fort was built inside the earlier one. The archaeological teams have revealed pottery from this period. It included mixing bowls from Gaul as well as storage vessels that would have contained olive oil from southern Spain. Pottery of a later date and defensive ditches suggest that the fort was occupied for about another 100 years, perhaps as a stopping point along the Roman road network for official travellers. A civilian settlement also grew up outside the fort. Consisting of timber buildings it was occupied only for a few years.

This fort at Metchley was on the line of another significant Roman road – the route from the south west which came via Gloucester, Worcester and Droitwich and which followed the modern Bristol Road South and Bristol Road into Bournbrook. Hutton certainly exaggerated the importance of Birmingham before 1166, even though his Ikenield Street may well have gone along Icknield Street; but he was right in pushing forward a Roman presence locally.

The two routes proposed for the Roman road of Icknield Street may well be both right and represent separate roads, and there is also evidence of farms from the Roman period in Kings Norton and Sutton Coldfield – and of pottery manufacture in Perry Barr. More tantalisingly, shards of Roman pottery found in Moor Street and Park Street give a hint of perhaps a Roman farm in the Bull Ring area. All roads may have led to Rome, but some Roman roads led to Birmingham.

Inge Street and Phillips Street, City

Birmingham was one of the greatest manufacturing towns in the world during the nineteenth century. Brummies declared with pride that wherever you found man or woman, from the icy wastes of the Arctic to the deepest jungles of Africa, there too would you find Birmingham because even in the most remote regions folk would be using something made in Brum.

A host of industrialists from a variety of backgrounds made their fortune from manufacturing the goods wanted by the world – from Matthew Boulton to Joseph Chamberlain, and from Joseph Lucas to George Cadbury. Yet for all their wealth, manufacturers like these were not as rich as the families that owned the land upon which houses, shops and factories would be built and through which were cut roads, canals and railways.

The Goughs, later the Gough-Calthorpes, found their treasure not in the production of buttons, brass, pens or the like but in their ownership of most of Edgbaston and part of Perry Barr. Similarly the Gooch family from Wrentham Hall in Benacre, Suffolk increased their riches through buying agricultural land in Highgate, Brookfields and the town centre; whilst the Digbys and Legges waxed wealthier through their inheritance of the Holte estates in Aston and Small Heath.

Merchants like the Colmores may have made their money through trade but once it was gained they used it to buy land and become 'gentlemen'. So too did the Rylands, who transformed themselves from manufactures to landowners in Sherbourne, Warwickshire as well as in Ladywood and Sparkhill. And so too did the Gillotts, whose pen making business in the Jewellery Quarter financed the purchase and development of the Rotton Park Estate.

Amongst the wealthiest of the landowning families of Birmingham were the Inges of Thorpe Constantine in Staffordshire. Recalled in Thorp Street (strangely it is spelled without the 'e') and Inge Street, they owned much of the City Centre through their relationship to the Phillips family, who had a long connection to Birmingham and its district. They had land in Erdington from before 1250 and in

A rare shot of Phillips Street. Taken in 1958 from Worcester Street, it shows the old Market Hall on the right. As the sign indicates, demolition was soon to sweep away all these structures, along with Phillips Street itself and the rest of the old Bull Ring. The only feature that remains is The Times building, now Waterstone's.

1285 an Adam Phelyp served as a juror in the growing market town of Birmingham, which had been founded just over 100 years before. In the succeeding centuries, each generation of the family seemed to grow more prosperous.

Some nineteenth-century historians state that the Phillips's were 'among the Jewish families who, coming from Normandy at the Conquest, were enabled to purchase land'. Supposedly called Filippes, this name would suggest that if they were Jewish then they came from the Iberian Peninsula, where there were large numbers of Sephardi Jews. However, it is impossible to prove these assertions.

Whatever their origins, the Phillips's did very well. In 1426 a John Phelyps was described as a chalonnere, signifying someone who sold a kind of blanket. Birmingham then was a town where the production of cloth was important, and it was through selling such goods that the Colmores also made their fortune. However, by 1463 a William Filippes is given as an attorney and 90 years later a William Phillippes is mentioned prominently in a great survey of Birmingham. In 1553 he held freely one dwelling house in the street called 'Dygbathe', with a croft (an enclosed piece of land for tillage or pasture) and two pools (fish ponds).

He also had land and buildings in Park Street, which were close to an ancient stream called Hersum, or Hassams ditch. This may have been important for supplying water to wash yarn and flax for the family's earlier business, and it also fed the pools down below in Digbeth. Additionally William rented land and buildings in Moor Street (then called Molle Street), New Street, High Street, Dale End and elsewhere. One intriguing rental relates to that of a pasture called Bennetts Hill, for which William paid one rose at the feast of the Nativity of St. John the Baptist only.

William lived at Earl's Barton, near Wellingborough, but his two sons, Robert and Ambrose resided in Birmingham, as had done their ancestors. They seem to have been the last to have done so. Ambrose inherited the family lands and he is later described as a gentleman living in Walsall. No longer having to work to earn their money, the Philips family had become gentry.

By the early seventeenth century the Phillips now owned most of the land and dwellings that once they had rented, as well as much of New Street and the Bull Ring. In 1692 a copy of lease of land from Robert Phillips, then of Newton Regis near Tamworth, to John Jennens named 'Phillips his Street'. This Phillips Street eventually ran from the bottom end of High Street along the side of the old Market Hall and into Worcester Street. Robert also held two large pieces of land stretching towards Bull Street called Banner's Croft and the Horse Close. His wife, Elizabeth, later gave the Horse Close for the building of St. Philip's Church, which was consecrated in 1715 and which commemorated her husband; and also for the building of the Blue Coat School, founded in 1724.

The Phillips direct line died out with Robert and through marriage with a female heiress, his lands passed to Theodore William Inge of Thorpe Constantine. Between 1753 and 1825 various acts of Parliament allowed building on the Birmingham estates. The family continued to own much of Inge Street until 1956, when Mary Caroline Inge sold her properties to pay death duties.

Bordering on part of the Gooch Estate, Inge Street appeared un-named on a map of 1781. It was thus a relatively new street when it was home to the young George Jacob Holyoake in the 1820s. An avowed campaigner for the rights of working-class people and a historian of the Co-operative Movement, Holyoake evoked an almost village-like feeling in his memories of Inge Street.

The grime of smoke, of decay and comfortlessness were not then upon it, rather it was fresh and bright. Before the Holyoake's door at number 1, stood a 'considerable clump of well-grown trees, amid which was a hatter's working shop'. On the adjacent corner of Hurst Street stood the Fox Tavern, as it stands now, and below which was a 'Green'. At the bottom was a garden belonging to a house with a gateway, where one of Holyoake's aunts lived. The garden fence was not a dead wall, 'but a low, wood paling, through which children could see the flowers in the garden'. From the end of Inge Street the trees of the parsonage of St Martin's 'made a small wood before us, and apparently in their midst, but really beyond them, arose the spire of the "Old Church". On summer afternoons and moonlight nights the church spire, rising above the nestling trees, presented an aspect of a verdant village church in the midst of the busy workshop town.'

Down through the "Green," the way led to Lady Well Walk, where more gardens lay, and where the well was wide, clear, and deep. Writing at the turn of the twentieth century, Holyoake averred that 'Inge Street, now, looking down from the Horse Fair end, is, as it were, the entrance to a coal-pit, which, when I first knew it, appeared as the entrance to a sylvan glen'.

By then, Inge Street and its district were dominated by shops, back-to-back courtyards and small workshops. It was known as 'Little Jerusalem' because of the large number of Eastern European Jews who had settled hereabouts. Tailors, glaziers, shoemakers and others they were a hard-working, clean and respectable people who had been forced to flee the Russian Empire because of persecution. As for nearby Thorp Street it was best known for its barracks, from which many men of the Royal Warwicks went to war in 1914.

Eventually the housing was cleared and Jews and non-Jews moved out. Inge Street became part of Birmingham's theatre quarter, dominated by the Hippodrome, and now lies on the edge of the Arcadian and the Gay Quarter. Yet amidst this new Birmingham there lies the last courtyard of back-to-backs in Birmingham. A National Trust property that harks to the past, it brings to the fore the hardships and vital contributions of all those Brummies, whatever their creed or colour, who should be remembered as much as the wealthy families of our city.

Inkerman Street, Aston

Colonel Thomas Unett was a valiant soldier and a man who should be better remembered in Birmingham. Born in 1800 at number 6, The Square – the Old Square – he was the son of John Wilkes Unett, a Lichfield man who became a solicitor here and a landowner around Aston and Hockley, hence **Unett Street**. Running between Great Hampton Row and New John Street West, Unett Street was always pronounced as Unit Street by Brummies. In his powerful attack on the exploitation of children as workers in 1905, the writer Robert Sherard dedicated a chapter to 'Child-Slavery in Birmingham'. In it he drew to mind a woman of 90 whom he had met in 'Unit Street'. Her eyes had the glaze of approaching dissolution upon them and her hands were knotted and labour-gnarled. Yet 'her eyes had been bright once. She, too, had brought industry and energy to the miserable tasks in which her life began. Years had followed years, decade had added itself to decade. There had been no change brought by chance or time.'

Thomas Unett by contrast had a very different life. He was a military man who served with the 19th Regiment of Foot in the Crimean War. Damned by Field Marshal Lord Montgomery as 'one of the most ill-managed campaigns in all recorded history', this pitted the Russians against the British, French and Turks – whose chief aim was to capture the major naval base of Sebastopol and so destroy Russia's supremacy in the Black Sea.

The British and French forces gathered at Varna in Bulgaria, where they were devastated by diseases, and after which Varna Road, Edgbaston was called. Thence in late September 1854 they were shipped to the Crimea – about which the British led by Lord Raglan knew little. Remembered by a **Raglan Road** in Edgbaston and Handsworth, the commander was an administrator who had never led so much as a battalion into action and was chosen because he was the only officer on the short list who was under 70! As the British and French moved towards Sebastopol they were attacked at the River Alma. Despite blunders by Raglan, the bravery of the British troops and officers ensured a victory hailed by the naming of **Alma Street**, Aston;

Looking up from Inkerman Street on the left to the Barton's Arms in High Street Aston. Like nearby Alma Street it was cut out of meadows soon after the Crimean War. Much of the local land was owned by Mr Potter and Mr Whitehead – hence **Potters Hill**, **Potters Lane**, and **Whitehead Street** and **Whitehead Road**. This development was called Aston New Town, leading to **New Street**, because old Aston village was around the church of St Peter and St Paul and Aston Hall. By 1884 New Town was a ward within the then independent town of Aston. It had a population of about 9,000 crammed into just 57 acres and its own shopping street, High Street, Aston – better known as Newtown Row. Albert Ketelby, one of the greatest British composers of light classical music, was born at 41 Alma Street. That street remains, although shorn in two, but Inkerman Street disappeared with the building of the Newtown Shopping Centre in the 1960s.

Alma Crescent off Dollman Street, Vauxhall; **Alma Passage**, off High Street, Harborne; and **Alma Place**, off Stoney Lane, Sparkbrook.

Approaching Sebastopol, the British captured the small port of Balaclava, making it their chief supply base. Then on 25 October the Russians attacked the British and Turkish defences. The incompetent British staff sent a muddled order to Lord Cardigan to lead his Light Brigade in a suicidal charge down the wrong valley to capture a battery of Russian guns. As they rode down this valley of death, the courageous cavalrymen came under murderous fire from three directions. Despite terrible losses, the guns were won. **Balaclava Road** close to Kings Heath Village honours those who fought in this most brave but needless charge.

Then on 5 November, the Russians launched another major assault covered by heavy fog. Greatly outnumbered and perhaps helped by the inability of their commanders to exercise control, the British troops repulsed the enemy at this battle of Inkerman. It is recalled in **Inkerman Street**, Aston and **Inkerman Street**, Vauxhall, which was cut out of Duddeston Meadows; whilst **Cathcart Street**, Vauxhall honours Sir George Cathcart, a leading British officer killed that day.

The British troops endured the hardships of a freezing winter without warm clothing or proper equipment, and were ravaged by cholera, dysentry and malaria. Thousands died and thousands more would have perished had it not been for the nursing skills of Mary Secole and Florence Nightingale, probably recalled in **Florence Road**, Kings Heath.

With the coming of Spring, British supplies improved and Sebastopol was attacked in a bloody failure by the allies in June 1855, soon after which Raglan died of cholera. Then on 8 September the French threw themselves at one massive Russian defence fortification called the Malakhov whilst the British strove to capture another named the Redan. That day Colonel Unett tossed a coin with Colonel Wyndham for the honour of leading his regiment in the assault. Unett won and lost his life.

The British sent just 3,000 men to storm a bastion manned by 12,000. As the attackers ran the great distance from our most advanced positions, the Russians devastated them with a terrible fire of cannon, musketry and rifles. Officers were a prominent mark for the defenders and Colonel Unett was one of the first to be hit: 'thus, after the long and laborious task, and in the hour of victory and triumph, he met a hero's death'. The British were repulsed with heavy loss of life, but fortunately the French captured their objective. The Russians had to abandon Sebastopol and their Black Sea fleet was destroyed.

Wearied by war, both sides anxiously sought peace. In Birmingham, a granite column was erected as tribute to the memory of Colonel Unett by his friends and townsmen. It is in Saint Philip's Cathedral churchyard and is dedicated 'to his memory as a record of the noble example of one who chose the foremost place in the path of duty with the calm undaunted spirit of a Christian soldier'.

Another Brummie who fought in the Crimea was Isaac Reeves. At the age of seven he was apprenticed to a copper plate printer for a shilling a week – from which his parents gave him a penny; but when still a mere youth he walked from Birmingham to London to join the Army. He was rejected as a little too short, so undaunted Isaac traipsed to Sheerness to join the Navy, whence he sailed to the Crimea on the 'Princess Royal'. He was then posted to the smaller 'Spiteful', which was ordered to close in during the attack on Sebastopol. The boat came under very heavy fire and was shot through the foremast, mainmast and below the water line. Later, Isaac went on the 'Spiteful' to Balaclava Harbour, up the Danube and back to the Black Sea. He was also to fight in Indian Mutiny and died aged 87 in 1923. (Thanks to John Reeves, Isaac's great grandson).

Institute Road, Kings Heath

Running off the High Street, Institute Road brings to mind the Kings Heath and Moseley Institute that was built on the corner of Alcester Road in 1878. An educational institution mostly for adult, middle-class men, it was similar to the Moseley and Balsall Heath Institute that was set up in 1877 as the Moseley and Balsall Heath Literary Association and which met at Tindal Street Schools. Six years later the M and B, as it became known, moved to the building still prominent on the Moseley Road between Brighton Road and Trafalgar Road. The heads to the windows on the ground floor are embellished with carvings representing Science,

A steam tram is coming up Kings Heath High Street towards Kings Heath Schools on the farthest corner of Institute Road. This is now the site of the shops and offices of Scotts Corner. On the opposite corner is the Kings Heath and Moseley Institute, later cleared for the building Woolworth's – not the present premises as they are a later development. The photo must have been taken before 31 December 1906 when steam trams stopped running in and around Birmingham after 24 years service.

Literature, Art, Music, Poetry and Drama; and on either side of the entrance are carved heads representing Michelangelo and Shakespeare. There was also a Perry Barr Institute, where the present Birchfield Library stands.

All three institutes were the focus of debating, literary and other societies aimed at intellectual activity. The Kings Heath building was on land given by the late Joseph Henry Nettlefold, who also paid £200 towards the building fund. His wife laid the foundation stone. A lecture hall was added in 1882, by which time the red-brick Institute boasted a library, newsrooms, and a large hall. It was also the venue for science classes and the Kings Heath Working Men's Club. The site is now occupied by Woolworth's.

Irving Street, Lee Bank/Attwood Green

Hailed as 'the father of American literature', Washington Irving could never have achieved his eminent position if it had not been for his visits to Birmingham. A patriot who had fought against the British in the War of 1812, yet Irving was a man attracted to the old world and three years later he joined his eldest brother in business in Liverpool. His hopes of success were dashed. The venture failed, along with so many others in the depression that swept the land with the coming of peace after the end of the Napoleonic Wars.

Dejected, Irving came to Birmingham to stay with his sister, Sarah, and her husband, Henry Van Wart, a prosperous merchant. Descended from the Dutch settlers who had founded New York as New Amsterdam, Van Wart had met his wife whilst working for the mercantile firm of her older brother, Irving and Smith. After a time in Liverpool and then back in America, they moved to the West Midlands, settling first on the West Bromwich Road, Handsworth, now the Soho Road, and afterwards on the corner of Newhall Street and Great Charles Street.

Then Van Wart purchased Springfield House in Icknield Street West, close to where Spring Hill Library would be built. That caused a problem. He had been born just months after the Americans had won independence from Britain in 1783 and so was an alien disbarred from holding freehold property. To overcome this, Van Wart obtained a special act of Parliament which naturalised him as a British Citizen.

Unsurprisingly, his income was gained through trade with his homeland, buying as he did large quantities of Birmingham goods and shipping them to New York. This was ended by the war of 1812 and Van Wart's enterprise collapsed. Not a man to be bowed down, he became a successful factor, selling for commission the products of small and medium sized manufacturers who could not afford salesmen, catalogues, or showrooms. In later years he also helped to start the Birmingham Stock Exchange and became a director of the Birmingham Banking Company.

By the time that Washington Irving came to Birmingham, the Van Warts were living with their four children in style at Springfield. Their house forever had happy associations for Irving as his 'English Home', the redoubtable castle of 'Van Tromp' – the playful name by which he called his sister's family. His nieces and nephews delighted in his company and he wrote of the happy 'romps in the evening between dinner and tea time, in the course of which I play the flute and the little girls dance. They are but pigmy performers, yet they dance with inimitable grace and vast good-will, and consider me as the divinest musician in the world; so, thank heaven I have at last found auditors who can appreciate my musical talents.'

Despite this cheerfulness, Irving was still downhearted about his future. One night Van Wart strove to raise the spirits of his brother-in-law by reminiscing about their childhoods in Irvington on the River Hudson. He rose up memories of strange characters, of queer goings on, of local stories and of funny incidents and Irving's thoughts turned back to his writing – for in 1809 he had brought out *The History of New York by Diedrich Knickerbocker.*

The urge to take up his pen once again grabbed him. In his bedroom, Irving's thoughts flooded out, almost too fast for him to put them down on paper. The minutes fled by and when the June sun dawned, Irving had written several chapters of a book. According to Elihu Burritt, later the American consul in Birmingham in the 1860s, Irving entered the breakfast room 'radiant with the old light of his genius and intellect. He came with his hands full of the sheets he had written while they were all asleep. He said it had all come back to him.' It was the enchanting world of his childhood, of 'Sleepy Hollow' that had indeed come back to him and he read aloud to his enraptured family the first chapters of *Rip Van Winkle.*

Soon after, the Van Warts bought a house on Camden Hill (later known as Newhall Hill), at the corner of Legge Lane and Frederick Street. Burritt visited it. By then it was enclosed in Wiley's Gold Pen Factory and surrounded by Messrs Fowler, Lancaster and Co., electrical engineers. He stood in the breakfast room and emphasised its importance to Irving's life. *The Sketch Book* was born there, though it received some of its development in other localities, whilst parts of his later novel *Bracebridge Hall*, was penned there. This took its inspiration from Aston Hall, features of which were jotted down in Irving's notebook of 1818: the gateway to Aston Park, 'studded nails, squirrel on top of gateway – gateway and porters lodge sheltered under trees... church spire rising above... Old oak gallery of great extent... figures of knights in armour with banners.'

Irving went on to travel in Spain and elsewhere, but he continued to visit Henry and Sarah Van Wart. About 1820 they moved to their seventh house in the newly-formed Calthorpe Road, close to Five Ways, and the author's stays there are recalled in the nearby **Washington Street** and Irving Street, which was called **Little Hall Street** until 1873. Henry Van Wart was recognised widely as a real gentleman. He took an active part in the public life of Birmingham, becoming a councillor, an alderman, and a borough magistrate. His wife died in 1848, but he lived until he was 1873, when he was ninety. The Van Warts and their bond with that wonderful writer Washington Irving should be brought to mind more often in the town they chose as home.

Island Road, Handsworth

Running from the Holyhead Road to the Sandwell Road, Island Road takes its name from a large building called Island House that was situated close to Sandwell Road.

J

Jaffray Road, Erdington

Jaffray Road and its extension of Jaffray Crescent go between Gravelly Hill and Wood End Road and highlight a major yet little-known figure in Birmingham's history. Born in Stirling, Scotland in 1818 John Jaffray came to occupy an influential position in the Midland metropolis where he settled. Educated at the public school in the town of his birth and at Glasgow High School, he became a journalist in Shrewsbury on a newspaper owned by a relative. Then, when he was 26, Jaffray arrived in Birmingham with £20 to start as a reporter on the *Birmingham Journal*, 'at a moderate salary'. This was a weekly paper and recently had been bought by John Frederick Feeney (see Frederick Road, Aston). An Irish journalist from Sligo, Feeney was an intensely private man and left behind little information for historians to learn more about him. By contrast, although Jaffray did court publicity neither did he shun it and unlike Feeney he played a pivotal role in the public life of Birmingham.

Strong, striking, determined, hard working and articulate, according to *Birmingham Faces and Places*, Jaffray speedily developed 'such abilities and such persistent industry', that he was taken into partnership by Feeney in 1852. The agreement gave the Scot a third share, with profits and losses in the same proportion. The *Journal* became Birmingham's principal newspaper 'and was noticeable for the able manner in which it was conducted, and the excellence of its style. In its later days it contained a perfect mass of news and instructive matter, and always appeared with a supplement.'

Then in 1855, the Government finally repealed the duties on newspapers which had made them expensive to buy and which had been designed to hinder both the journalists who supported political reform and the spread of radical ideas. The end of these 'taxes on knowledge' had long been campaigned for and their disappearance encouraged the emergence of daily newspapers, such as the *Daily Post* set up in 1857 by Feeney and with Jaffray as editor – although he later gave up that position to focus on the paper's commercial activities.

Jaffray played a crucial part in the rise of this newspaper and its 'high and richly-deserved reputation . . . standing as it does in the highest rank of provincial journalism, may with truth be said to be mainly due to the rare business tact, the untiring energy, the keen intelligence, and the strict adherence to principle displayed by Mr. Jaffray in its conduct and management'. As the *Daily Post* waxed so too did Jaffray. He became an active figure public life, so that there was 'scarcely any department of it which does not bear the impress of his efforts.'

It was said that everything he touched turned to gold and that he was the political kingmaker of the Midlands. A staunch Liberal who was firm in his belief in free trade in economics, society and religion, he was one of the influential group who asked

John Bright to stand as an MP in Birmingham (see Greens Village). Despite his
misgivings, he eventually followed Joseph Chamberlain away from the Liberal Party
and into Liberal Unionism, but he always asserted Liberal principles – as with the
Post's support of the Union in the American Civil War at a time when many English
newspapers backed the Confederacy.

In particular, Jaffray was drawn to the thorny topic of education and in 1850 he
joined the Birmingham School Association. At this time there was no national system
of schooling and most poor children either did not go to school or attended Ragged
schools or those run by the Church of England. Challengingly the Association
campaigned for the introduction of a free, secular, and compulsory system of national
education that would be supported by local rates. Jaffray was also prominent in the
foundation of the Birmingham and Midland Institute, the objectives of which were to
provide educational facilities for working men; and in pushing for the establishment
of the Birmingham Free Libraries. Indeed he was one of the members of the first
Libraries Committee elected from outside the Town Council.

A Life Governor of King Edward's School, and a justice of the peace, Jaffray was
one of the founders and first directors of the Birmingham Joint Stock Bank,
established in 1862, and became its chairman. He was also chairman of Muntz's
Metal Company for a time, and had extensive commercial affairs locally. His activity
in business affairs was matched by his work for charities in which he took 'a
prominent and effective part. One of the founders of both the Children's Hospital and
the Women's Hospital, he was a governor of the General Hospital – with which
institution 'his careful, conscientious, and princely benevolence are widely known'.

Through his connection with the General Hospital, Jaffray 'was led to entertain
the idea of founding the Suburban Hospital which bears his name, and which will
carry down to future generations the story of his munificence'. The Jaffray Hospital
in Wood End Lane, Erdington came about because 'it was found that in consequence
of the numberless accidents in a town like Birmingham such pressure was put upon
the resources of the Hospital that the authorities were obliged to put some period to
the detention of patients who otherwise they would wish to keep in the wards'.

Accordingly in 1883 Jaffray offered to pay £15,000 to provide a suburban
hospital for the free reception of chronic cases. He secured eight acres of land 'in an
elevated situation at Gravelly Hill, and built upon it, at his own cost, the best building
for the purpose that could be devised. It was erected by Messrs. Wilson, of
Handsworth, from designs by Mr. Yeoville Thomason. The institution was erected
and furnished solely at Mr. Jaffray's expense, and through his influence an
endowment of upwards of, £36,000 was secured'. Opened by the Prince of Wales
'with great *éclat* on the 27 November 1885', the Jaffray's fourth wing was opened by
the Duke of Norfolk on 25 July 25 1888.

At his home of Park Grove in Edgbaston, now part of the Priory Hospital, Jaffray
had 'a fine collection of pictures, including specimens of Louis Haghe, Rosa
Bonheur, E. K. Johnson, David Cox, Henry Moore, and other painters of celebrity'.

His great interest in art led the philanthropic Scot to be a trustee of the Public Picture Gallery Fund and to take 'a great interest in the establishment and furnishing of the Art Gallery'. Indeed it was thanks to him and his friendship with Cox that the City acquired the Warwickshire Drawings of the Birmingham painter.

Described by a friend 'as a curious mixture of shrewd commercialism and kind-heartedness' Jaffray retired in 1894 aged 75, by which date he was living at an estate near Redditch. The article on Jaffray in *Faces and Places* concluded by declaring that 'there is scarcely any philanthropic or educational agency in the town of Birmingham which has not at some time or other received benefit and assistance from Mr. Jaffray. While he has grown rich and honoured, he has not forgotten the needy and the afflicted. In whatever aspect he is regarded it must always be felt that he is one of Birmingham's foremost citizens.' He died in 1901, by which time he had been knighted and made a baronet.

Jakeman Road, Balsall Heath

Cutting through from Edward Road to Willows Road, Jakeman Road may be named after a Job Jakeman who was a farmer living in Balsall Heath in the 1850s. Diane R. Rivers is a Jakeman by birth and her brother, Michael, has researched the family history and believes that there had been a Jakeman Farm in the district for a considerable number of years.

James Turner Street, Winson Green

James Turner was a Birmingham gun barrel manufacturer who tenanted Holford Mill, Handsworth on the bend in the River Tame above Witton in the 1850s and 1860s (see Holdford Road). It seems unlikely that this road was named after him. There was another James Turner, who was minister at Cannon Street Baptist church from 1754-80. This was regarded as the 'mother' church of Baptists in Birmingham. Turner was instrumental in firmly establishing Baptists locally.

James Watt Street and James Watt Queensway, City

It was a momentous meeting that day late in August 1768 when James Watt decided to visit Matthew Boulton at Soho House in Handsworth: a meeting that was momentous not only for the two men but also for the world. A Scot from Greenock, Watt's probing mind and mathematical aptitude were enhanced by his deep thinking and determination to apply scientific principles to his enquiries. A master of problem solving, Watt's thirst for knowledge was all embracing and led him to grasp philosophy and learn German and Italian. An intellectual of the highest order he was also a talented craftsman whose deft hands were attuned to mechanical endeavour.

After a tough start learning to become a mathematical instrument maker, Watt became a successful businessman in Glasgow. Keen to expand his knowledge and his income, he became involved in a pottery company. But it was not through these endeavours that Watt was to make his mark upon history; rather it was through his investigations into the steam engine. Contrary to popular belief, Watt did not invent the steam engine – his genius lay in developing the steam engine into an effective form of power that was crucial in propelling Britain into becoming the world's greatest industrial nation.

Essentially a steam engine is a machine which uses steam to convert heat energy into mechanical energy. For centuries men had striven to perfect the steam engine and by the mid-eighteenth century the most common in England was Newcomen's, which was designed to pump water from mines. The steam came from a boiler that was filled with water and beneath which a fire was lit, hence the early steam engines were also known as fire engines. Above was a cylinder, open at the top, and in which the steam was condensed by a jet of water. Thus contracted, the cool steam pulled down a piston that was attached to a long beam, at the other end of which was a red pump rod. The beam itself was rocked down so that the pump was raised. Its weight then lifted the beam back and began the process again.

Unfortunately Newcomen's steam engines needed an excessive amount of steam, which meant a waste of fuel. Watt discovered this was because the piston and

A rare photo looking down into James Watt Street. Is it the 1930s? On the right is Birmingham Billiards on the corner of Corporation Street, billiard cue and ball makers; whilst opposite is the Army Recruiting Offices in James Watt Street itself. At the bottom street on the right is the Bell Tavern, which was on the corner of Dale End, and beyond which is Coleshill Street.

cylinder cooled during every stroke and then had to be reheated. He recognised that he needed a way to condense the steam without cooling the cylinder. For more than two years Watt wrestled with the problem and then in May 1765 as he took a walk on a fine Sabbath afternoon he was inspired: 'the idea came into my mind that as steam was an elastic body it would rush into a vacuum, and if a communication were made between the cylinder and an exhausted vessel it would rush into it, and might be there condensed without cooling the cylinder. I then saw that I must get rid of the condensed steam and injection-water if I used a jet as in Newcomen's engine.'

Watt's concept of a separate condenser was brilliant and was based upon an appreciation of latent heat, whereby the steam cylinder remained hot while a separate condensing vessel was cold. This meant that the condensation process could take place constantly.

Over the next few years Watt eagerly worked on his steam engines. It was costly. Although he was also employed as a surveyor for a proposed canal in Scotland, his debts mounted, leaving him little choice but to go into partnership with Dr John Roebuck. A doctor who had practised in Birmingham, Roebuck was also a chemist who had moved into the production of sulphuric acid and the ownership of iron works and coal mines in Scotland. Roebuck took over Watt's debt of £1,000 and insisted that his junior partner should go to London to protect his invention. Watt took the oath patent for 'A new method of lessening the consumption of steam and fuel in fire-engines' on 9 August 1768. Roebuck owned two thirds of it. A fortnight later Watt set off for home, stopping at Soho to meet Boulton.

Later hailed as one of the industrial geniuses of the world, Boulton was already on the way to becoming a world figure. The owner of a superb manufactory at Soho, two miles north of Birmingham town centre, Boulton made steel gilt and fancy buttons, ormolu, steel buckles and many more toys – small metal goods. A skilled worker and inventor himself, Boulton was as adroit at public relations, marketing, managing and helping others to realise their dreams and ambitions.

The two men clicked. Impressed by Boulton's vim and vigour, by the prowess of his workers and by the scale of his manufactory, Watt extended his stay by two weeks. He later wrote 'I explained to him my invention of the steam engine, and several other schemes of which my head was then full, in the success of which he expressed a friendly interest'. As for Boulton, he was keen to become involved with Watt and was not ashamed to proclaim his motives, declaring to the Scot that he was excited 'by two motives to offer you my assistance which were love of you and love of a money-getting ingenious product'.

Unfortunately it took several years before Watt was able to extricate himself from his other partnership and join forces with Boulton. But at last he arrived in Birmingham in May 1774. A year later the wily Boulton gained an act of Parliament to extend Watt's patent for another 25 years and within a month the Boulton and Watt partnership had begun. Boulton was to be the financier, general organiser and publicist, whilst Watt was do what he did best – make drawings and surveys and direct the project.

The first steam engine at the Soho Works was soon running and on 11 March 1776 the Bentley Mining Company began using a Boulton and Watt engine. *Aris's Birmingham Gazette* reported that: 'From the first Moment of its setting to Work, it made about 14 to 15 Strokes per Minute, and emptied the Engine Pit (which is about 90 Feet deep and stood 57 Feet high in Water) in less than an hour'. The pumping out of water from coal mines was vital if the mines were to be sunk deeper. Similarly, water had to be pumped out of the tin mines of north Cornwall and Boulton and Watt found a ready market for their engines here; but Boulton was certain that the steam engines could do more than pump out water and he encouraged the ever self-doubting Watt to develop his ideas, writing to his partner that 'The people in London, Manchester and Birmingham are steam mill mad. I don't mean to hurry you, but I think in the course of a month or two, we should determine to take out a patent for certain methods of producing rotative motion . . . There is no other Cornwall to be found, and the most likely line for the consumption of our engines is the application of them to mills which is certainly an extensive field.'

Watt did produce rotative motion so that wheels could be turned. He and William Murdock, (see Murdoch Road) invented the sun and planet gear system, whereby one or more outer gears, or planet gears, rotate around a central or sun gear. This was better than a crankshaft which was already patented, and which Watt said was an idea stolen from him. It also allowed the rotative wheel to turn more than once per stroke of the piston. Steam engines could now drive machinery in factories and Boulton and Watt sold many to textile industrialists.

Watt continued to improve his engines, bringing in valves above and below the piston; he devised a mechanism to match the arc-like rocking motion of the beam with the linear motion of the piston; and he came up with the steam throttling valve and the mechanism to connect the throttle to the engine governor. Importantly, many of the parts of the early engines were bought from suppliers in the Midlands, especially John Wilkinson. Known as 'iron mad Wilkinson', by the 1790s he had eleven Watt engines at his Bradley iron works in the Black Country. Jennifer Tann, an expert on Boulton and Watt, reckons that a total of 449 engines were manufactured by Boulton and Watt for the British market alone. In this way, the Boulton and Watt steam engines accelerated British industrial growth.

Gradually Boulton brought about an increase in the amount of parts made 'in house' – especially after the development of the Soho Foundry in 1796 in Smethwick, just across the border from Birmingham and Handsworth. Four years later, Watt retired from an active part in the business.

Matthew Boulton died in 1809 aged 81.Watt said of his great friend and encourager that 'few men have had his abilities and still fewer have extended them as he has done'. Watt himself died in Handsworth on 25 August 1819 and was buried beside Boulton in St Mary's Church, Handsworth. A statue of him was erected to his memory in Westminster Abbey. The inscription was by Lord Brougham and it encapsulated the gifts of Watt.

Not to perpetuate a name which must endure while the peaceful arts flourish, but to show that mankind have learned to honour those who best deserve their gratitude, the King, his ministers, and many of the nobles and commoners of the realm, raised this monument to James Watt, who directing the force of original genius, early exercised in philosophical research, to the improvement of the steam-engine, enlarged the resources of his country, increased the power of man, and rose to an eminent place among the most illustrious followers of science and the real benefactors of the world.

When he had first come to Birmingham, Watt had lived in Boulton's old home at Newhall Walk, but soon he moved to Regent's Place on Harper's Hill in what would become the Jewellery Quarter. In 1790 he authorised the building of a new home in Handsworth called Heathfield House. Above the kitchen was a garret which he used as his workshop. In the succeeding years Watt acquired an estate of 40 acres. The house was later residence of the famous engineer, George Tangye. It was demolished in the mid-1920s after the Gibson Watt trustees developed most of the Heathfield Park Estate, hence **Heathfield Road**. The Brecon Tennis and Bowling Club leased part of the land and that was built upon in the 1950s. **Wattville Road** also connects to James Watt, ville being the French word for town.

Jenkins Street, Small Heath
Running from Bolton Road to the Coventry Road, Jenkins Street recalls a John Jenkins who owned the Small Heath Meadow and Small Heath Field according to the 1845 Tithe Apportionment Map. This land was occupied by a Henry Jenkins. In 1855 an act of Parliament was passed that authorized building leases on certain parts of the estate of the late John Jenkins of Saltley Hall. Jenkins Street itself was cut in the 1880s.

Jephcott Road, Alum Rock
In his undated manuscript on 'Birmingham Street Names' for the City Surveyors Department, A.H. Bevan states that this road was named after a city councillor. It comes off the Alum Rock Road just along from the Brookhill pub and goes into **Jephcott Grove**. I have been unable to find out anything about Councillor Jephcott.

Jennens Row, Duddeston
In a wonderful drama, the successful BBC series 'Bleak House' brought to a television audience the powerful and poignant novel by Charles Dickens. Its aim was to assail the futility of longstanding law suits that destroyed lives and fortunes through all-consuming legal bills, and to highlight the folly of those embroiled in such hopeless litigation. The book's plot hung upon the interminable case of Jarndyce v Jarndyce, the result of a contested will, which had ground down generations of claimants. As Dickens despaired, 'Jarndyce and Jarndyce drones on. This scarecrow of a suit has, in course of time, become so complicated that no man alive knows what it means.'

Fictional as it was, the case of Jarndyce and Jarndyce was not mere fanciful thinking. It is probably based upon the real case of Jennens, Willis v Earl Howe – and therein lies a strong connection to Birmingham. The name Jennens was a most important one in the growth of industrial Birmingham. By the sixteenth century Digbeth and Deritend and some surrounding settlements were well known for their metal workers, and in 1586 Camden in his "Britannica," declared that 'Bremicham' was 'swarming with inhabitants, and echoing with the noise of anvils, for the most part of them are smiths'.

These scythe smiths, nailers, bladesmiths and others bought their raw material of bar iron from middlemen – to whom they also sold their finished wares. Such ironmongers were vital in marketing our products across the nation. Of them all, the Jennens family was the richest.

William Jennens was an incomer. In 1560 he married Joan Elyott, who belonged to a prominent Birmingham family. An inn holder he was highly successful through his low rental of valuable properties in the town and in 1602 he left considerable holdings. William's sons, John and Ambrose, became ironmongers and traded extensively and profitably with London. John had a grand house in High Street and secured his own supply of iron through forges at Bromford Mill and Aston. This latter had belonged to William Cowper, hence Cowper Street, and was recalled in the intriguing Furnace Lane by Porchester Street.

John's eldest son by his second marriage was Humfrey. He and his wife, Mary, moved from the family's High Street mansion to Erdington Hall, which they rented

Jennens Row in the 1930s, showing the empty premises at number 1 of J. Ball, paper merchants. Thanks to Geoff Dowling.

from the Holtes and where they lived in lavish style. In Birmingham, Humfrey owned the land to the east of Masshouse Lane around Saint Bartholomew's Church; and in later years he added to his wide estates with the manor of Nether Whitacre and Gopsall Hall in Leicestershire, recalled in **Gopsal Street**.

Humfrey and Mary had twelve children. Of these, a younger son, John, carried on the family business in Birmingham, which ended with his death in 1733; whilst the family estates in Gopsall were passed to the oldest brother, Charles. His son, another Charles, was a noted patron of the arts, owner of a peerless musical library and outstanding art collection, and a great admirer of the celebrated classical music composer, Handel. Indeed it was Charles Jennens who wrote the libretto, the text, for the magnificent Messiah by Handel. Sensitive, moody and prone to depression, Charles died childless.

As remarkable a personality was his first cousin, William – the last male of the line of Humfrey Jennens and reputedly the richest commoner in England. William's father, Robert, had been an aide-de-camp to the great Duke of Marlborough and in 1708 he moved to Acton Place in Long Melford, Suffolk. This was close to the home of his sister, Esther, who had married into a local family.

Miserly and uncaring of appearances, the bachelor William wore shabby clothes and spent as little as possible. He died in 1798 aged 98 and left no will. His landed property was calculated by some to be worth £650,000; he held £270,000 in stocks and shares; there was £247,000 at his bankers, in cash and dividends; and at his several houses, there was found close upon £20,000 in bank notes and more than that in gold. This was a fabulous amount. The money, shares and personal effects fell to the descendants of Humfrey's daughters, Hester and Ann. They were William Lygon, later 1st Earl Beauchamp, and the Dowager Lady Andover of Elford Hall, Staffordshire – brought to mind in Andover Street.

As for the landed estates of William in Birmingham and Suffolk, like those of his cousin, Charles, they were inherited by Richard William Penn Curzon because he was the grandson of Charles Jennens, the oldest son of Humfrey Jennens. Richard later became the 1st Lord Howe through his mother, Sophia. These family connections led to the naming of **Penn Street**, **Curzon Street** and **Howe Street**.

This settlement dismayed and angered the numerous distant cousins of Jennens. Showell's History of Birmingham explained that from 1810 'the collaterals and their descendants have, for generations, been fighting for shares, alleging all kinds of fraud and malfeasance on the part of the present holders and their predecessors, but the claimants have increased and multiplied to such an extent, that if it were possible for them to recover the whole of the twelve million pounds they say the property is now worth, it would, when divided, give but small fortunes to any of them.'

At various times there were supposed to seventeen legal proceedings in operation, the last of which was on behalf of American claimants and which was thrown out of court in 1934. It was these law suits that are supposed to have inspired Jarndyce v Jarndyce in Bleak House by Dickens – a tale that comes to full attention through the name of Jennens Row.

Jervoise Road, Weoley Castle

Going between Weoley Castle Road and Kemberton Road, Jervoise Road brings to mind the Jervoise family. In 1531, the manor of Northfield and Weoley was sold by the Dudleys to Richard Jerveys. A wealthy mercer and holder of the important office of Sheriff of London, he was recognized as someone 'of grete power and having grete substance'. He did not live at the fortified manor house of Weoley Castle and instead leased it to John Churchman of Northfield; whilst the park was leased to John Statham (see also Ledsam Street).

Jiggins Lane, Bartley Green

Running up from Adams Hill to Clapgate Lane, Jiggins Lane is named after the 'Gyggans Medewe' of Medieval times. Who or what was Gyggans is not known. For most of the nineteenth century there were a few cottages at the bottom of Jiggins Lane, close to Clapgate Lane, a few more half way up the hill by the smithy, and then another small gathering of houses by the 'Cock Inn'. Thence was the steepest part of the hill, which led to Bartley Green Village at the coming together of Genners Lane, Field Lane, Brook Lane, and of course, Jiggins Lane itself.

Bartley Green was noted in the Doomsday Book of 1086 as Berchelai. This means either the birch tree wood or the clearing in the birch trees (from the Anglo Saxon 'beorc leah'). Sited on a ridge of boulder clay between Stonehouse Brook and Kitwell Brook, hence **Kitwell Lane**, Bartley Green belonged to the manor of Weoley. It remained an agricultural settlement until the early twentieth century, although its

Frontages to houses on the new estate in Clapgate Lane in 1969. The road skirts the tress on the left and is hidden by the mud.

population grew slowly but surely in the later nineteenth century. As a result in 1840, the village gained its own church, that of St Michael and All Angels. It was a chapel at ease to the parish church of Northfield.

In 1878 a piece in the *Harborne Herald and Smethwick News* stated that the small population of Bartley Green was mainly nailers and labourers. One Bartley Green resident who gained unfortunate fame was Jane Bumford. At 7 feet 7 inches she was the tallest woman in the world and would have stood higher but for a spinal abnormality. Her length had been caused by damage to her pituitary gland when she received a head injury when she was eleven years old. Jane's family lived in a nailer's cottage at the top of Adams Hill and then in Jiggins Hill. Nearby was the home of a friend, a small woman called Little Emma Kinver. Jane herself died in 1922.

Another well known local resident was Jane Wells Webb. Her father, Thomas, was a Birmingham manufacturer who bought Kitwell Farm (also called Kitwell House) in 1820 after his wife's death. Both the farm and the brook may hark back to Peter Kytte who was mentioned as living locally in the 1275 subsidy rolls and who gave his name to a well in this area.

Four years after moving to Bartley Green, Thomas died leaving Jane an orphan aged seventeen. Later in her life she recorded how after her fathers death 'and, finding on the winding up of his affairs that it would be necessary to do something for my support, I had written a strange, wild novel, called the Mummy, in which I had laid the scene in the twenty-second century, and attempted to predict the state of improvement to which this country might possibly arrive'.

Because of the prevailing domestic ideology which dictated that a woman's place was at home and that she had no right to enter public life as could a man, Jane published her book under the pen name of a man. *The Mummy* was set in 2016 and although a fantasy it was a perceptive about changes to come. Amongst other things Jane wrote of the replacement of feather beds by mattresses with elastic springs; air-conditioned houses; mass produced shoes and clothes; and a steam engine for milking cows – the concept of which captured the attention of John Loudon, a well-known landscape gardener and writer on gardening. Jane was to marry him.

At 47, Loudon was 24 years older than his bride, but they forged a powerful partnership. Jane threw herself into the world of gardening, growing roses and peonies with her husband and helping him with his experiments with plants. Soon she was his secretary, copyist, researcher and note taker, and she played a key role in his massive work, *Encyclopaedia of Gardening* (1834). However, Jane herself was to make her mark on gardening enthusiasts. She claimed that books on the subject were too technical and so wrote *Instructions in Gardening for Ladies*. Clear and accessible and including personal sketches of and stories about gardeners, it pushed forward gardening as something suitable for ladies and sold more than 20,000 copies.

She followed this with *The Ladies Flower Garden* (1839) and other books. However, by now her husband's fortunes and health had declined and he died thirteen years after their marriage. Widowed at 36 with a young daughter, Jane survived on a pension of £100 granted from the Civil List 'in recognition of the literary services rendered by herself and her husband'. She never re-married, but continued to write books, including *Tales for Young People*, which recounted the animal stories she had heard when she visited France. Jane died in 1858 aged 50 and was buried next to her beloved husband. Their daughter, Agnes, went on to write several children's books.

At the time Jane Webb lived in Bartley Green it was still a remote rural locality. Bartley Farm was on Scotland Lane and Genner's Farm was close to the junction of Genner's Lane and Woodcock Lane. South of them lay Bromwich Wood and to the west was Kitwell Farm. Change was heralded in 1911 when Bartley Green became part of Birmingham along with the rest of Kings Norton and Northfield.

A few years back, Cyril McCoy wrote to me with wonderful memories of the old Bartley Green. He was born in Devon Street, Nechells, opposite the old gas works in 1913, but at two weeks old the family went to live at Bartley Green because his mom came from there.

Cyril well remembered:

the hard times. We lived in a small cottage in Jiggins Lane next door to Billy Young the blacksmith. In those days there were plenty of characters about all with nicknames: Billy Pug, Katy Andrew, Piggy Statham, Billy Whistler, whom it was said made his own wooden teeth and his wife, Little Emma and Jinny Mumford the giant who never went out, always sat in the window.

The McCoy's cottage had a stone floor and no hot water, gas or electric. It was lit by paraffin lamp held on the ceiling with chains, which had to be pulled down every day to fill the lamp with paraffin and to clean it. The toilet was about 100 yards up the garden 'and the night soil men used to come and empty it during the night. Imagine what it was like during the night in the winter'.

Once the village constable caught Cyril and Kenny Kendrick scrumping apples in Brett's Orchard and 'he gave us a cuff round the ears, took us home and told our moms and dads, then they gave us another one, but it never did us any harm. It's a pity they don't do it now as manners are a thing of the past'.

There were no buses to Bartley Green until about 1931 or 1932 when Cyril's father instigated the Number 12 running there:

through his friendship with Councillor Billy Hodge, the man who built the Northfield Cinema. I shall never forget the first number 12 bus coming. It was one Wednesday evening in the summer and it was an open top double decker. We all cheered like mad. I remember the driver till this day. He was a very chubby country fellow named Tishy Blick and he came from Harborne. He ran to the top of Jiggins Lane and I'll never forget the Cock Inn was open and Tishy coasted the bus down to the Cock and Billy Moody the gaffer came out with a pint and Tishy drank it as sweet as a nut and went on his way.

John Coulson was the grandson of Billy Moody. He kept the Cock Inn for about 30 years until he retired in 1946 and 'my mother Lillian Coulson (nee Moody) lived there until she married in 1936 and was the local music teacher. She lived in Bartley Green all her life, first at no. 18 Jiggins Lane and then at 228 Jiggins Lane until she died in 2000.' John still holds fast the memories of Bartley Green before the village was transformed by the developments of the 1950s.

> I can remember watching the wheelwrights (Inston's?) in Jiggins Lane fire the metal tyres on wooden wheels and the local blacksmith, Albert Young, making horse shoes and shoeing the horses. There were many working farms in the area that they named new housing estates after, i.e. Athol House Farm and Kitwell Farm. In the original village there were five shops – Andrew's the grocer's, Whittingham's the butcher, Hudson's general stores, Callaghan's the greengrocer's, and Moss's the Post Office. There was also a café with a barber's shop upstairs.

Attending St Michael's School with Miss Treadwell as the headmistress, John also went to the youth club in the church hall, which had been the headquarters of the Home Guard in the Second World War. Today Newman College stands on the site. The original St Michael's School had only three classrooms, one next door to the café and two across the road and opposite the old St Michael's Church, which is no longer there. Next door to the school was the doctor's house, which was empty for years and the fire station. This had a water tower which gave its name to Tower Stores, the local hardware shop. A block of flats now occupies that spot at the junction of Jiggins Lane and Field Lane.

Developed both with private and council housing, Bartley Green was finally transformed in the 1970s when the corporation laid out a large estate at Kitwell. Yet with the great Bartley Reservoir and its green surrounds, Bartley retains a powerful feel of the countryside.

Johnstone Street, Ladywood

The connection between Monument Road and St Vincent Street, Johnstone Street seems to hark back to the Dr John Johnstone, who was associated with setting up Fever Hospital and was its first consulting physician in 1828. He was based on the corner of Bishopsgate Street.

Johnson Road, Aston

Going between Station Road and Oliver Road, this may be named after Alderman Alfred Johnson JP, who was an electro-plate manufacturer on the Aston Road and who was chairman of the Aston Board of Guardians – the workhouse for which later became Highcroft Hospital.

K

Kent Street North, Winson Green

Ted Rudge runs a cracking web site on Winson Green and comes out of this street. He has done much research into its origins and tells me that fits original name was Foster Street, as recorded on the Pigott Smith Map of 1855. Foster Street was laid out after Norton Street, which was an established street off Lodge Road and named some time in the fifteen years between Bradshaw's Plan of Birmingham of 1840 and Pigott Smith's. However, the first official mention found was that of Kent Street North in the 1866 *Post Office Directory of Street Names and Places*, with no mention of a Foster Street. As Birmingham had already got one Kent Street in the centre of the town the naming of a second followed by North may simply have been deliberate or a corruption of Norton the adjoining street?

Key Hill, Hockley

Stretching up from the junction of Lodge Road and Icknield Street to the merging of Great Hampton Street and Great King Street, Key Hill in Hockley was once known as Kaye Hill – and it is likely that it is called after Sir Arthur Kaye, the husband of Anne Marrow. The Marrows had bought the manor of Birmingham in 1555, after the last of the de Berminghams, Edward, had lost control of his lands. Anne and her sisters were the last of the Marrows and about 1730 they disposed of their inheritance to Thomas Sherlock, later Bishop of Birmingham – recalled in Sherlock Street and Bishop Street.

Sherlock's sister, Mary, was his heir. She was married to Sir Thomas Gooch, who lived at Benacre Hill in Wrentham, Suffolk – giving rise to Gooch Street, Gooch Street North, Benacre Street, Wrentham Street and Suffolk Street (see Gooch Street). The East Anglian connection was made even plainer by the cutting of Norfolk Street, off Suffolk Street, which was demolished in 1886 as part of a major redevelopment of Birmingham City Centre.

Sir Thomas was aware of the growth of Birmingham and realised the potential in the development of the local estates that he had inherited. However, in his will 'the pious old' Bishop Sherlock had forbade any building both in his lifetime and thereafter, because he believed that the land was 'valuable, and if built upon, his successor, at the expiration of the term, would have the rubbish to carry off'. Undeterred, Sir Thomas set aside Sherlock's wishes by an act of Parliament that allowed him and his sons Thomas, William and John and their guardians to grant building leases of certain areas.

This move led to the slow urbanization of the Gooch land between Bristol Street and Gooch Street, where Hope Street and Vere Street perpetuate the name of Harriet Hope Vere, the second wife of Sir Edward Sherlock Gooch, the sixth baronet. The

Looking up Key Hill in the 1950s from Lodge Road, 'The Flat'.

Gooch family also owned land in Brookfields; along Broad Street, where they leased six acres to the Birmingham Canal Navigations for their wharves; and in Bordesley, leading to Benacre Drive off Fazeley Street.

As for Key Hill, it referred to a hill itself and to a short and steep street that was obvious on maps from the mid-eighteenth century – although as far down as Warstone Lane the rest of the bank was sandpits or gardens. These were probably some of the allotments for which Birmingham was well-known and were located on the skirts of town. In plots of an eighth or a sixteenth of an acre they were rented for either a guinea or a half guinea a year for the growing of vegetables.

By the early 1800s and as Brum moved onwards, Branston Street and Spencer Street had been cut out of that part of Key Hill owned by Colonel Vyse – hence Vyse Street; while Forest's Brewery was obvious on the corner of Icknield Street and Warstone Lane. In the middle years of the century these premises were taken over and turned into the works of the world famous Birmingham Mint.

The rest of the slopes of Key Hill stayed as small gardens until the 1830s when a company took over the ten acres of the land which ran down from what was to become Key Hill Drive. About 1,200 people paid £10 each for shares so that the spot could become a General Cemetery. Walks, lawns and shrubberies were laid out, catacombs were cut into those parts which were sandstone rock and a chapel was built for the burial services. Beneath it were the living quarters of the registrar. The cemetery opened in April 1836 and within a few years Pitsford Street, Northampton Street, Hockley Street and Augusta Street had also merged on the Vyse Estate. Then 1848 the remainder of Key Hill was bought from the Gooch family by the Church of England Cemetery Company.

Just across Pitsford Street from its rival and consisting of sixteen acres extending down from Vyse Street, the new cemetery boasted an ingenious system for the transfer of the deceased from St Michael's Church, in which the burial services were held. The bier was placed in the middle on an ornamental stand in the middle of the nave, from which a hydraulic machine lowered the coffins to the vault. From here they were carried along underground passages to circular catacombs.

By 1854 the two cemeteries were effectively divided by Birmingham Wolverhampton and Dudley Railway, which brought to Key Hill part of Hockley Goods Station. The slopes appeared to have almost disappeared behind walls and beneath buildings – although the hill was still brought to mind by the street at its north-western tip. Small as it was, Key Hill came to have a strong significance for the Brummies of Hockley, Winson Green and further afield.

Its top end was packed with enamellers, jewellers and die sinkers, but the retailers of its lower part merged into those of 'The Flat' of Lodge Road so as to form one of the major shopping thoroughfares in Old Brum. There were two expansive drapers – Tim's and Nortons, who also had a house furnishing store across the road – as well as smaller shopkeepers like Mrs Pittam the tobacconist and Rose Pitt the huckster. They've now gone, like so many of the shops of Brummagem past and like so much of the hill itself, but the historic name of Key Hill is carried on by that short and steep street.

King Edwards Road, Ladywood

Called Lower King Edwards Road until 1884, King Edwards Road used to go down hill from Cambridge Street, across Monument Road and up to Stour Street. Now it is split in two. The top still starts at Cambridge Street, at the back of the ICC, and runs alongside the National Indoor Arena, which dominates the west side of the street. It then stops at the island which brings together St Vincent Street and Clement Street and across from which is Summer Hill Street. The drastic transformation of Birmingham's landscape in the early 1960s cut off this upper portion by the building of Nelson School and St Mark's Crescent. Thus the bottom end of King Edwards Road is a pudding bag street, cul-de-sac, that runs just a short distance from close to the bottom of Anderton Street and into Ladywood Middleway (formerly Monument Road) – and no longer goes on to Stour Street.

Truncated as it may be, King Edwards Road highlights one of the most important institutions in Birmingham and one of the most longstanding and important landholdings in the city – King Edward's School. Today the King Edward's Foundation still owns much of Ladywood and elsewhere in the city centre and it is regarded by many as the pre-eminent educational establishment in the city – and all success that is derived from the Middle Ages.

On 25 October 1382, Thomas of Sheldon, John Colleshull, John Goldsmith, and William ate Slowe applied for a licence to endow two Chaplains who should celebrate divine service daily 'in honour of God, our Lady his mother, Holy Cross, Saint Thomas the Martyr, and Saint Catherine, in the Church of St. Martin of Birmingham'. It seems that it was granted but was not put into effect. Consequently, a decade later, the bailiffs and the commonalty of the town of Birmingham themselves sought a licence from the Crown to found a Gild and perpetual fraternity 'of brethren and sustern' in honour of the Holy Cross.

This Gild was open to men and women both within and without Birmingham, whilst its members could appoint a Master and Wardens to govern it, found a chantry, and do other works of charity. John Colleshull, John Goldsmyth, and William atte Slowe were allowed to assign to the proposed Gild, eighteen messuages, three tofts (house), six acres of land, and forty shillings of rents, in Birmingham and Edgbaston. An inquiry was held to ascertain whether the formation and endowment of such a gild would injure anyone. The jury, which included John and Thomas Phelip (see Phillips Street), found positively and reported that those making the endowments held their

A cracking photo of the corner of Monument Road and King Edwards Road in the late 1950s and showing how safe it was for children to be out and about on the street. The newsagent at 404 is 404 Thomas James Dickins and the chemist next door is that of Ronald George Pharo. The remaining premises in that block are James Henry Price, fried fish dealer; Ernest Harold Yale, radio engineer; Mrs. Winifred Alice Forrest, draper; Summer Hill Methodist Church; and the local children's day nursery.

property or lands from the lords of the manors of Birmingham, and Edgbaston – the de Berminghams and Middlemores (see Middlemore Road).

The Borough of Birmingham paid £50 for the licence, and the Gild of the Holy Cross then built its hall – with its clock and chimes – at the bottom end of New Street, where the Odeon now stands and where King Edward's School used to be. It came to be a wealthy organisation, receiving gifts of land and buildings across the borough, the built-up part of Birmingham, in and around the Bull Ring, Dale End, Bull Street (then called Chapel Street), New Street, High Street, Moor Street (then known as Molle Street), Park Street and Deritend. Additionally the Gild owned land, pasture and houses in the foreign, the rural part of Birmingham.

In his fascinating book on the *Men and Names of Old Birmingham* (1864), Toulmin Smith revealed that the Gild 'being musical, had an organist, William Bothe', who had 'a handsome salary. They had also a clerk of the Gild, whose name is unhappily not recorded in its proper place'. Furthermore a Thomas Groves was keeper of the Gild House, or Town Hall as it was called, and its gardens – for which service he lived rent free in two of the Gild's cottages. Finally there was an officer called the Belman. However, there was no school. This facility was provided by the Gild of St John the Baptist in Deritend.

Still the Gild of the Holy Cross itself was a wide-ranging body, a kind of a trust that was funded by wealthy folk and which became vital for the physical wellbeing of Birmingham's people as much as for their souls. However, all religious bodies fell under suspicion after Henry VIII broke with the Pope and the Catholic Church in 1533. Three years later, the king began to dissolve the monasteries and to take over their property for the Crown. The end seemed nigh for Gilds as well, but in 1545 the royal commissioners made favourable reports upon them. With regard to Birmingham they stated that the town had many poor people whom the Gild 'found, aided and succoured . . . as in money, bread, drink, coals'. When the need arose, the Gild also paid for the burial of the poor 'very honestly' with a dirge and mass.

Moreover, it funded three priests at the parish church of St Martin's, a local midwife, almshouses, and maintained and repaired two great stone bridges and 'divers foule and daungerous high wayes, the charge whereof the towne of hitselfe ys not able to mainteigne; so that the Lack therof wilbe a great noysaunce to the kinges majesties Subjectes passing to and ffrom the marches of wales, and an utter Ruyne to the same towne, being one of the fayrest and most profitable townes to the kinges highnesse in all the Shyre'.

Unhappily, the Gild was not reprieved for long. In 1547, commissioners reporting to the new king, Edward VI, declared that gilds were religious foundations that that had to be broken up and their lands and monies confiscated. Undaunted, the next year leading Birmingham men, amongst them the High Bailiff Richard Smalbroke, petitioned the king for the return of some of the Gild's funds so as to endow a school. They achieved their aim and in the 57th of the Certificates of King Edward VI it was stated that 'the saide Towne of Brymyncham ys a very mete place, and yt is very myte and necessarye that there be a Free Schoole erected to bring uppe the youth, beig boathe n the same town and nigh thereaboute'.

Named after King Edward VI himself, the school gained its charter in 1552 and was endowed with part of the possessions of the Gild of the Holy Cross. The grant of lands to the school totalled about 125 acres and included 'all those fields, meadows and pastures, and hereditaments, whatsoever with the appurtenances, called or known by the name or names of Long-Croft, Bynges, Rotton-fields, Walmores, and Saint Mary Wood lying and being in the Foreign of Birmingham'. King Edwards Road, Ladywood was to be cut through the Saint Mary Wood area.

The school itself was run in the old Gild Hall, which was pulled down about 1731 and replaced by a new building. Then in 1833 the Governors applied for an act of Parliament to allow a complete rebuilding. They were successful and engaged Charles Barry to design it. He went on to find fame as the man who brought us the Houses of Parliament. Barry's Gothic structure of Derbyshire stone was ready in 1838. It was imposing and had seven ranges of windows in front. That wonderful building was knocked down in the later 1930s after the Governors sold the site for £400,000 and King Edward's moved to Edgbaston.

The school is also commemorated in **King Edwards Drive,** Ladywood and King Edwards Place, which went between Broads Street and Cambridge Street. It ran parallel with King Alfred Place which was also on King Edward's Trust land and at 468 feet above sea level was the highest point in the central part of Birmingham. Both disappeared when the ICC and Symphony Hall were developed in the 1980s. There was also **King Street** that came off New Street and the line of which is now followed by **Stephenson Street**, and was named after the nearby King Edward's School in New Street. **King Edwards Close** and **King Edwards Gardens** in Handsworth relate to King Edward VI Handsworth School, established as a girls' school in 1911.

Kings Road, Kings Heath

Coming off Vicarage Road and like the adjoining Kings Close and Kings Terrace, this takes its name from the district in which it is located. The earliest reference to Kyngesheath is from 1511, and eight years later Humfrey Stafford granted John Middilmore an annual rent of a messuage (dwelling house with out buildings) and land on the heath called Kingsheth in the parish of Kings Norton. Another deed from 1541 also mentions Kyngisheith as lying close to the land of Bartholomew More. Taking its name from the royal manor of Kings Norton, to which it belonged, the heath lay across the modern High Street. This is confirmed by the Act of Parliament which allowed the extension of the turnpike road to Alcester in 1767. This was the forerunner of the Alcester Road and the law mentioned that the route would pass over Kings Heath.

By the early nineteenth century, Kings Heath was little more than a hamlet. It had a Baptist Chapel on the High Street from 1816, local offenders were tried at the 'Cross Guns' or the 'King's Head' at Alcester Lane's End, and toll gates halted travellers. The slowly growing population could also worship in All Saint's Church from 1859, but there was no industrial activity of importance. Most of the folk were farm workers or engaged in small handicrafts – although there were a few wealthy families living in grand houses. Amongst them were Major Howard Cartland (see Cartland Road) and J.H. Nettlefold. He lived at Kingsfield, hence **Kingsfield Road**, now the site of Saint Dunstan's Catholic Church. Kings heath was developed into a populous suburb from the late nineteenth century (see also Grange Road).

Kings Road, Kingstanding

Bringing together the Queslett Road and Kingstanding Road, Kings Road was previously known as **Coffin Lane.** Before the Kingstanding Estate developed, the lane was narrow, so narrow that two vehicles could not pass along it, with the result that coffin-shaped lay-bys were made for one vehicle to move into so as to allow the other to go by.

Kingstanding Road, Kingstanding

Kingstanding: in the 1930s it was one of the newest estates in Birmingham, showing off roads that were freshly cut out of farmland and designed in circles, horse shoes, semi-circles and curves and which were lined with modern houses that boasted electric lights, hot water, bathrooms and proper lavatories. With such mod cons it is no wonder that young couples with children were drawn to Kingstanding and away from the decaying back-to-backs of Aston and Summer Lane.

A wonderful photo of the Circle at Kingstanding in 1949, with the splendid Art Deco Odeon on the left.

So rapid and overwhelming had been the urbanisation of Kingstanding that it was as if its rural roots had been torn out of the earth and banished for ever from the area. Yet here in a district that is so much a product and a part of Birmingham's recent past is a mound that is one of the city's oldest man-made monuments. There it is on the Kingstanding Road, close to Sutton Oak Road, almost imperceptible except for a slight rolling rise and a tree at each end. No more than a yard in height and about twenty–two yards in length, it is circled by a slight trace of a ditch, from which the earth would have been dug to make it. And who did make it? It seems that they were prehistoric men and women, from either the later stages of the Neolithic Age (New Stone Age) or the early Bronze Age.

This would date the mound to some time before 1,700 BC. Between 3,800 and 4,800 years old then, it is probably a barrow, a burial mound. No-one knows who was laid to rest beneath the earth and little is known about the people who carried out this funeral rite. Neolithic flint tools have come to light in Sutton Coldfield; whilst a Neolithic polished stone axe was discovered when Deritend High Street was widened in 1953, and others have been found at Minworth and Northfield.

The flint originated from the south and east of England, and the stone for the axes came from the Lake District. This seems to indicate that the peoples who used them for felling trees so as to clear land for agriculture and for cutting wood for fires and buildings had wide trading links. Slight evidence such as this hints at a farming folk that were not passing through as had been the hunter gatherers of the Mesolithic Age

(Middle Stone Age). The earliest settlers locally they may have been but we know so little about them – not their language, their religion, their attitudes or their social structure. But what they have done is left their mark, not only on the landscape but also in the name Kingstanding.

According to a popular story, however, Kingstanding gained its title during the English Civil War. In October 1642, King Charles I was heading from Shrewsbury to relieve Banbury Castle and decided to stop at Aston Hall. Approaching what is now The Circle, he reviewed his troops from a mound thrown up by his men. In 1930, George Podmore, the vicar of Hamstead wrote that twenty years previously, an old man of almost 80 had told him that when Perry Common had been enclosed at the start of the nineteenth century, the tenant of Kettle House Farm thus **Kettlehouse Road**, had brought horses, wagons and men to cart away the knoll. Lord Calthorpe was informed and came at full gallop from Perry Hall to stop it.

Another tradition explains that the tenant did remove the mound and found much treasure of silver chains. Upon learning of the story of King Charles, the farmer supposedly then built a new mound a short distance away and fenced it off. This is the present site on the Kingstanding Road. There is another more prosaic explanation that Kingstanding is derived from a standing – a hunter's station from which to shoot game. Given the proximity to the royal chase of Sutton, then this is plausible.

However the intriguing research of Ronald E. Crook brings us back to the real origins of the mound as a prehistoric barrow. He has shown that the word king was common in the names of fields locally before the Civil War. Crook suggests that Big King's Field and the others similarly named may have arisen from older tales about the burial of a royal person in the original mound. Such stories are common where there are such hillocks and one such in Small Heath led to the naming of Golden Hillock – the mound where gold was supposed to have been buried deep in the past.

Kingstanding's historical significance is heightened because it is one of the few areas in Birmingham through which Roman soldiers definitely passed along Icknield Street, also called Ryknield Street. In 1762, William Hutton, Birmingham's first historian, looked at the remnants of the ancient road at the Ridgeway. He was struck with astonishment. It was the grandest thing 'I had ever beheld; and was amazed, so noble a monument of antiquity should be so little regarded.'

By then, Kingstanding was part of Perry Common in the manor of Perry, as it had been from the time of King John. Although the common was enclosed in 1814, little else changed before 1928 when the district was incorporated into Birmingham with much of Perry Barr Urban District. There was a small population, just a few cottages in Warren Lane (Road) and Cross Lane (now Crossway Lane) and four farms: Warren Farm – through which **Warren Farm Road** now runs; Half Way Farm – unsurprisingly half way up the Kingstanding Road and close to Short Heath Road (now Hawthorn Road); Pool Farm, near to the top of the modern Cranbourne Road; and Kettlehouse Farm, just to the west of today's Kingstanding Circle, and which was previously called King's Vale Farm.

Quickly, the council seized on the area as an ideal spot for a large municipal housing estate. Using a London builder who named most of the roads after places in the capital and the south-east of England, the corporation provided 6,302 homes for 30,000 people by 1932. Many of the residents called the area Little Russia – because it was so high up that it caught the full blast of the cold winds from Russia which came across the plains of Poland and North Germany, the North Sea and eastern England.

The houses on the estate were well built and laid out attractively, but there were problems. Kingstanding's population was close to that of Shrewsbury, which had 30 churches, fifteen church halls and parish rooms, two public libraries, four picture houses and 159 pubs. By contrast, the Birmingham suburb had one church, one hall, one picture house and one pub. It had no parks, sports grounds or hospital. Now a maturing estate, Kingstanding yet calls out to us of the deepest origins of Birmingham.

Kingsbury Road, Erdington and Minworth

Named as Minworth Road in the Inclosure Ward for Erdington and Witton in 1804, Kingsbury Road starts at Gravelly Hill, goes across the junction of Wood End Road and Bromford Road, then over the Tyburn Road to pass Castle Vale to the south east. It then travels via Minworth itself and leaves the City boundary just before Broad Bank Bridge, eventually ending just south of Kingsbury.

Probably meaning Mene's enclosed farmstead, Minworth was a detached hamlet of the parish of Curdworth, from which it was separated of which it by a projecting strip of land belonging to the parish and borough of Sutton Coldfield. By 1883 Minworth had become a civil parish with an area of 1,525 acres, but in 1931 it lost its independence. Birmingham took over the Castle Bromwich Aerodrome section (see Castle Vale) and other land in the western portion of Minworth, totalling 585 acres; Castle Bromwich was given 189 acres in the south; and the remaining 751 acres in the northern and eastern portions of the parish were transferred to the parish and borough of Sutton Coldfield. This district included the sewage works of the Birmingham Tame and Rea Drainage Board and the village of Minworth. Along with the rest of Sutton Coldfield, this part of Minworth joined Birmingham in 1974.

The village is gathered about a green, to the south of the Kingsbury Road, which is all that is of the common. Minworth Church of St. George was dedicated by the Bishop of Birmingham on 23 October 1909, and its local junior and infant schools sees itself as Birmingham's last village school. As for Kingsbury it was originally *Chinesburie* and means a 'royal fortified house' or 'Kings Fort'. For many years Kingsbury Hall was the family home of the Bracebridges (see Bracebridge Street).

Between 1929 and 1932 a local building called Minworth Greaves was taken down and put back up in Bournville, where it is now open to the public along with Selly Manor. Minworth Greaves had been bought by George and Laurence Cadbury in 1911. It dates to about 1250 and originally stood between Curdworth and Minworth. Little is known about its history although it had a main hall and would have been the dwelling of a wealthy family. However by 1880 what had been a fine medieval house was converted into two homes which were in bad condition. It was considered beyond repair and everything that could be was stripped out and sold. All that remained were the main timbers, before the Cadburys stepped in.

Kingshurst Way, Kingshurst

Going from Fordbridge Drive to Silver Birch Road, Kingshurst Way remembers an ancient settlement. According to William Hutton, Kingshurst was once its own manor, although later it became part of Coleshill, which was recorded as a royal manor in 1086. This ownership is recalled in the name Kingshurst which means the wooded hill of the king, and as late as 1610 William Mountfort held the manor from the monarch by fealty (allegiance) and the rent of a red rose. William was descended from the de Montforts who had been lords of Kingshurst since at least the mid fourteenth century. His son, Sir Edward, passed away all his rights to the Digbys, the lords of Coleshill.

Although tied to Sheldon and Shard End by closeness and tenant farmers moving between the two, Kingshurst remained part of Coleshill until the later twentieth century when it was acquired by Birmingham after the City had bought the Kingshurst Hall Estate in 1952. The Hall itself had been built in the early eighteenth century and was lived in by Walter Townsend, whose father had moved there in 1876. A 72 year old bachelor and recluse, Walter had been born there and who now occupied just a downstairs room with his two dogs. A smallholder, he eked out a living by raising a few livestock and felt that his home was a 'grand place' that should have been preserved. Sadly it was not and was demolished in 1962.

From the mid-1950s, Birmingham's housing department took the opportunity to create a mixed development council estate which gave homes to over 7,000 people. Unfortunately, few facilities were provided for these Brummies. The first of them arrived to unmade roads, cement mixers, black ash and the onslaught of the town on the country. There was only one bus, the 168 Midland Red along the Chester Road, and a single block of temporary shops until the permanent shopping centre was completed early in 1959, and they were called the 'Lonely Exiles' by the *Evening Mail*. Since then proper facilities have been built and in the local government reorganisation of 1974, Kingshurst has been part of Solihull.

Kingswood Road, Moseley

Linking Brighton Road and the tail end of Sandford Road, Kingswood House takes its name from a large house that stood hereabouts.

Knights Road, Tyseley

Named after Knights Farm, originally Knights Road was Knights Lane. It comes off the Warwick Road opposite Wharfdale Road and goes into Sunningdale Road. This latter road is part of an inter-war estate council that was developed on Tyseley Farm, which was probably the same as Knight's Farm (see also Tyseley Road). The Kings Norton Map of 1894 shows the line of Knights Lane going down to Tyseley Farm but

It is most unusual to come across photographs of a road showing before and after it was developed, hence the value of these two shots of Knight's Farm, Tyseley and Knights Lane.

gives no name. The houses, then, were built between 1894 and 1914. They are good quality homes with front gardens, put up for the best-paid of the working class and the lower middle class.

Kyott's Lake Road, Sparkbrook

Coming off the Stratford Road just past the bridge before Camp Hill, this was pronounced by Brummies as Koyts not Ki-otts. On Beighton's Map of 1722-4 this locality is given as Foullake, and it seems because a family called Kyott later lived here that the lake was called after them. A Kyotts Lake House was built on Cole Bank Road in Hall Green, on the stretch now part of Southam Road. It was changed to Cambrai House and is the site Hall Green Secondary School.

A rare shot of Tram 679 in 1953 in Kyotts Lake Road, where there was a tram depot. This was the last tram to move to the depot on the last day of tram operation in Birmingham. The tram was later broken up for scrap, along with almost all other Birmingham trams. The 'Black Horse' pub is on the right. This wonderful photo was taken by Dennis John Norton, a most talented and thoughtful photographer who captured Birmingham on the cusp of change in the late 1950s. It is included in an important new book in which his photos are contrasted with those taken by his son, Mark, which show the same spot today. the book is called In My Father's Footsteps, Birmingham Past and Present (Sutton Publishing 2006).

Kyrwicks Lane, Sparkbrook

Curving round from the Moseley Road to the Highgate Road, this is one of the most baffling street names in Birmingham. I have found references to it in the nineteenth century as called Hardwicke's Lane and Skirt's Lane, but I have no idea what it means.

L

Ladypool Road, Sparkbrook

Steeped in history, the Ladypool Road once was a country route and is still called 'The Lane' by older folk from the neighbourhood. Indeed it was Ladypool Lane until 1883 and for centuries it had run all the way from the old 'Angel' inn on the Stratford Road to Moseley Village but in 1855 the stretch from just above Brighton Road to St Mary's Row was changed to Church Road – because the wealthy of Moseley wanted to show their separateness from the working-class folk of Sparkbrook and Balsall Heath.

The origin of the name Lady Pool is the stuff of local legends. When I was a youngster in the 1970s, a chap called Fred Hubble who came out of Chesterton Road told me that when he was a child:

> of a Sunday Dad'd take us to an herbalist and botanical beer seller opposite Runcorn Road. He sold sarsaparilla, dandelion and burdock. While we there one time, an old man told us about the brook which ran down Church Road, along Taunton Road into the Spark in Stoney Lane. He was a very old, gnarled man with a stick. He said there had been a pool at the top of Church Road by St Mary's in which a lady had committed suicide. That's why the road's called Ladypool.

Another story states that the lady killed herself in a pool where the Carlton Picture House was to be built in Taunton Road. There is a more prosaic explanation, however. St Mary's is dedicated to Our Lady, Mary the Mother of Jesus, and hence the pool by the church was Our Lady's Pool – leading to the name Ladypool Lane. For generations the district through which The Lane ran was rural and many of its fields were rented out to drovers so that they could rest their cattle and fatten them up before selling them in Birmingham's market.

There were, however, three proper farms: one called after the Stoney Lane with its house close to where Brunswick Road would be cut out; another named Ladypool Farm, owned by the wealthy Simcox family and near to the bottom end of what would become Saint Paul's Road; and the last known as Old Farm, by Alder Road and on the edge of Moseley.

Growing up in the 1870s, my own great-grandparents lived in and about White Street and they recalled the Spark still flowing along the Stoney Lane, as it did until it was culverted at the dusk of the nineteenth century; and they brought to mind the hedgerows along the Ladypool Lane between Alfred Street and Brighton Road. My Great Uncle Wal recollected that they alluded to Sparkbrook 'as a pretty little village, describing the open country on both ides of the Stratford Road'. But as they became adults, my great-grandparents witnessed the wholesale urbanisation of the Lane.

Urban development had actually begun after the death of Thomas Mole in 1831. He was a wealthy manufacturer who had lived at the Poplars by the 'Mermaid' on the Stratford Road, hence **Poplar Road**, and his land was cut through with **Mole Street** and **Thomas Street** – which later became that part of the Highgate Road between the Ladypool Road and Stoney Lane.

The building of houses along the two new streets went on slowly but within twenty years there were two more developments. The first was around Clifton Road and the second took in **Queen Street**, **Victoria Street** (called **Studley Street** from 1897), named after the monarch, and Alfred Street – named after the son of one of the landowners, the Reverend Timothy East. Short and narrow, Victoria Street was filled with yards of back-to-back highlighting members of the Royal Family like Albert and Alexandra; whilst Queen Street had a distinctive terrace known as **Ten House Row**, which was bombed in the Second World War.

The slow encroachment of Birmingham was heralded not only by the emergence of these new streets but also by the appearance of the brickworks of Baines and Pidgeon on the Ladypool Lane and of the Birmingham to Gloucester Railway in 1840. Running to the east of what would become the Moseley Road, the railway embankment almost cut off the Lane from Balsall Heath and so ensured that it would have its own identity.

Nevertheless development was plodding. The Larches Estate was still dominated by a great house built by William Withering, the doctor who discovered digitalis, and the Sparkbrook races were run on a nearby field in 1857 and 1858. However, they had to move to a new course opposite the 'George' on the Ladypool Road with the break up of the estate and the cutting of **Spark Street** (after the Spark Brook), King Street and **Larches Street**. During the same decade the Birmingham Freehold Land Society laid out Hertford Street, Malvern Street, Brunswick Road and **White Street**, remembering John White a leading member of the Society who had played a prominent role in the purchase.

In the succeeding years houses appeared upon the land of George Marshall Turner, leading to **Turner Street** and **Marshall Street**, whilst the fields of Ladypool Farm and Stoney Lane Farm – where Sam Melson had 'a quaint old' house, fertile fields and 'his small stud of horses' – were overlaid with new homes. Urbanisation swept across the district in the 1890s, digging up the land for Chesterton Road, Colville Road, Leamington Road and others on the Stoney Lane side of the Ladypool Road and Kingsley Road and more on the other. Here **Ombersley Road** was named after the place in Worcestershire and **Oldfield Road** after the Oldfield Inn in that village. The bottom part of Oldfield Road was cut out first on the small plot owned by Henry Ludlow and was called Henry Street until 1892. Ombersley Road was also called Mug's Row because many of its houses were built by the Draysey Brothers, who also constructed the Hippodrome. They had made their money from bookmaking on the racecourse and so built Ombersley Road with 'mugs' money'.

This photograph was given to me by the late Raymond Jones, one of the Jones's the greengrocers, and a man who was highly regarded by all of us from the Lane. It shows Raymond's father, other relatives and local kids at the 'George Show', a small fairground that used to be at the back of the George pub, where the single storey shops are now. The family's vardo, caravan, is in the background, although the Jones's later moved into Alfred Street as did my Grandad, Alf Chinn. Raymond himself went to school with Our Dad and he was a proper Brummie, a real character whom I was proud to know from when I was a babby.

Rural Sparkbrook disappeared and a lively working-class neighbourhood took its place. Of 39 roads in the new district, all but eight led directly off the Lane or else were branches of such roads. Not surprisingly this position made the Lane the pulsating shopping artery for the neighbourhood, from Highgate Road upwards. It had butchers galore like 'Bonehill the Poor Man's Friend'; famed greengrocers such as Jones's and Westwood's with their motto 'Nuf Sed'; mouth-watering pork butchers of the calibre of Lunn's; tantalising sweet shops such as that of Mrs Hudson; succulent cooked meat shops like Mrs Cash's; colourful hawkers; tempting grocers; tasty bread shops; and bustling pubs. It even boasted 'The Olympia' picture house, a school, a Congregational Chapel and St Barnabas's Church – and, of course, it was the local monkey run. Those noted retailers have long gone but Ladypool Road remains a vital road. Now the heart of the Balti Triangle it continues to pull in folk from all around.

Ladywood Middleway and Ladywood Road, Ladywood

Trees abound in modern Birmingham. Along our streets, canals and railway lines and in our parks, recreation grounds, gardens and open spaces, trees strike upwards, bringing colour and shade, splendour and simplicity, wildlife and tranquillity to a big city that otherwise would struggle to find these qualities that enhance the lives of its citizens. Trapping sooty particles and absorbing poisonous chemicals, trees improve the air that we breathe and help all those affected by the Brummie disease of asthma. Their leaves and branches form umbrellas to catch rainfall and lessen the risk of flooding as much as they soften sounds, whilst their roots grasp hold of the soil and hold it fast from erosion.

Already one of the most treed cities in Europe, there are exciting plans to bring up to 100,000 new trees to Birmingham in the next four years. Vital both for the present and the future of our city, trees have also been crucial in our history and are highlighted in the very first document that refers to Birmingham. The Domesday Book of 1086 captured the state of England for a William the Conqueror who had taken the English crown twenty years before. The entry for Birmingham read that Richard held the manor from the mighty William Fitzansculf of Dudley. Along with the land that was in cultivation there was a wood that was half a league long and two furlongs broad. A league was about one and half miles in this period, giving about 120 acres by that calculation.

At just under 6,000 acres, Birmingham then was a much smaller place than it is today, but in the nearby manors that would later be drawn into our city woodland was as obvious. In Aston the wood was extensive at three leagues in length and half a league in width; in Erdington it was a league long and half a league across; whilst in Edgbaston it was smaller and stretched for just half a league. Woodland was also a prominent feature in Northfield, Frankley, Selly and Mackadown (Sheldon). Indeed place names with 'ley' endings emphasise the woodland setting for they are from the Anglo-Saxon word 'leah' meaning a clearing in the woods. Much of the woodland was probably wood pasture, where trees were set amidst grazing land, or else it was coppicing – whereby thickets of small trees (coppices) were regularly cut back to produce new growth.

Eighty years after Domesday, Birmingham gained its market charter and thenceforth it grew not only as a trading town but also as manufacturing town. Wood from local trees was important for fuel and for the building of houses – be they so humble as a farmstead or so grand a structure as Aston Hall. It was also essential in the smelting of iron before the introduction of coke.

Wood was cut down and then charred in hearths that did not allow in air and so prevented it from burning. This charcoal was then sold to iron smelters in Staffordshire, until furnaces began to emerge around Birmingham in the sixteenth century. In turn the smelters sold the metal to those who worked it – in places like Birmingham, as was revealed in about 1543 by John Leland. He came to the town and was struck by the large numbers of smiths who made knives and all manners of cutting tools, by the loriners who made bits for horses, and by the nailors.

The butcher's shop of Mrs Ada Marin Smith on the corner of Ladywood Road and Saint Vincent Street in the early 1950s.

The supply of iron to these fashioners of metal must have required a great amount of charcoal from the cutting down of many trees. One source outside Staffordshire may have been Sutton Coldfield, given that the Domesday Book entry for the manor suggests that there were almost 3,000 acres of woodland there compared to about 180 acres in Northfield. This assumption is strengthened by the meaning of the name Coldfield. It signifies the open land (field) where charcoal (col) was burned.

Despite the voracious needs of the smiths of Birmingham woodland had not disappeared locally. In 1529, a Survey of Birmingham mentioned a 'pasture or wood called the Worston', which was probably close to the modern Jewellery Quarter and has led to the naming of Warstone Lane. This was a small wood compared to one nearby and which may have been the wood mentioned in Domesday.

In 1552 King Edward VI signed a charter which set up the grammar school which carries his name still and which now is situated in Edgbaston. The new establishment was endowed with part of the possessions of the Gild of the Holy Cross, which had been dissolved during the reign of Henry VIII. The grant of lands to the school included 'all those fields, meadows and pastures, and hereditaments, whatsoever with the appurtenances, called or known by the name or names of Long-Croft, Bynges, Rotton-fields, Walmores, and Saint Mary Wood lying and being in the Foreign of Birmingham'.

Bynges was the area from which Bingley Hall would take its name; Rotton-fields was the land between Monument Lane and Summer Hill; the Walmores was the locality through which Walmer Lane (Lancaster Street) would run; and bearing the name of Our Lady, the mother of Christ, was Saint Mary's Wood – which came to be called Ladywood.

The word Foreign applied to the rural parts of Birmingham and is first documented in the thirteenth century – as is the word borough. This was where Peter de Birmingham and his heirs granted burgage tenure to anyone who wished to take it up. Held for a rent of normally 8d a year, burgage plots gave the owner an opportunity to build a house with a workshop behind, as well as privileged access to the market of Birmingham. These liberties and customs marked out the burgage holders from the rural folk of Birmingham.

For centuries, the borough of Birmingham was confined to the south east corner of the manor around the Bull Ring and down to Digbeth and Deritend, and the foreign was by far the greater area – although it was less important. West of the red sandstone ridge upon which the borough was sited, the foreign was mostly poor land of sand and gravel which was mostly covered in trees or heather and was regarded as a waste.

Until the early seventeenth century, the town of Birmingham was still huddled about Saint Martin's Church, but in the succeeding years the increase in population encouraged landowners to raise their incomes by granting building leases. Those parts of the foreign closest to the borough were soon swallowed up. However, Ladywood was a distant spot and remained deep in the countryside as was shown in 1690 when John Hinckley bought 79 acres and a good barn in Ladywood.

Along with the rest of western Birmingham, Ladywood was mostly not shown on eighteenth-century maps, however a map of 1810 brought to the fore the whole of Birmingham – town and country. It names Ladywood Lane as leading down from Five Ways. That stretch later became Ladywood Road and is now the Ladywood Middleway. However, it shows Ladywood Lane as continuing on to bend east and carrying on to the junction of Summer Hill and Spring Hill, where Spring Hill Library now stands. That part of the lane later became Monument Lane and then in 1878, Monument Road (see Monument Road). At one time Ladywood Road was also known as **Russell Row**.

For all the rapid growth of Birmingham in the next few years as late as 1825, Drake in his Picture of Birmingham explained that the further 'we recede from the Town there is no want of wood', whilst 'noble elms' still existed in Ladywood until 1848. Thereafter the last traces of the ancient woodland of Birmingham were chopped down and Our Lady's Wood was to be recalled only in the name of one of Birmingham's working-class heartlands – Ladywood.

Lancaster Street, City

Originally this was the lower part of **Walmer Lane** and on Hanson's Plan of Birmingham in 1785 it is shown as Walmer Lane or Lancaster Street. It would seem to have taken its name from the county town of Lancashire about the time that the Newtown Row neighbourhood was developed and that the lower part of Walmer Lane

A tremendous photograph taken from the clock tower of the Central Fire Station in 1957 following the terrible Halford's fire and after the skeleton of the building had been demolished, leaving an empty triangle of space dominating the shot. In the foreground is Corporation Street and to the left is Lancaster Street. The buses are coming along Brickkiln Street and are going into Lench Street.

was renamed Newtown Row (see Newtown Row). In keeping with the 'Roses' theme, **York Street** was also cut out of land nearby and which had been known as the Crossfields in the 1500s. York Street became **Lawson Street** in 1898.

Langley Road, Small Heath

Going from the Coventry Road to Glovers Road, Langley Road commemorates either a local landowner or the Birmingham artist, Walter Langley. As a city Birmingham has produced a number of artists of note, including the famed David Cox. Renowned for his paintings of landscapes in Wales and elsewhere, Cox was the son of a highly-skilled blacksmith from Heath Mill Lane. His depictions of the Bull Ring in the 1820s and of Crescent Wharf are wonderful illustrations of a Birmingham that can only appear to us in paintings and engravings.

Like Cox, Langley was belonged to a working-class family. Born in 1852, he was the eighth of eleven children. His father, William, was tailor and he and his wife, Mary Ann, lived in Irving Street. Langley was educated at the Unitarian Domestic Mission School in Hurst Street. This charged 2d a week to parents, which was too much for the poor but was within the reach of a skilled man like Langley's father. Langley himself was apprenticed to a lithographic printer when he was thirteen but his strong-willed mother was determined that he should have a chance to develop his talents and get on and. She took in washing to pay for her son to attend evening classes at the Birmingham School of Design. He must have been talented and shown aptitude, for in 1873 he was awarded a scholarship to study at the South Kensington Schools of Art.

When his scholarship ended, Langley went into partnership with Mr Biermann the Birmingham lithographer to whom he had been apprenticed, and in 1876 he married Clara Perkins. Unlike so many working-class couples they were able to afford a honeymoon. They spent it in Whitby. This was a favourite haunt of Victorian artists and gave Langley his first glimpse of life in a working fishing village. Returning home, Langley had to face a slump in the lithographic trade. Pulled back to a three day working week, hew was able to devote more time to his painting and began to gain attention as a commercial painter. Three years after his marriage, he abandoned his job for a life of painting.

Soon after he made this life-changing decision, Langley made his first visit to the Cornish fishing village of Newlyn. Then in 1881 Langley was one of six young artists chosen as the first Associates of the Royal Birmingham Society of Artists. That summer he returned to Newlyn with a commission for twenty paintings from an important Birmingham patron, Edwin Chamberlain. Later that year he received another lucrative commission from the Birmingham art dealer J. W. Thrupp, who was acting on behalf of the Alldays family. This gave him £500 for a year's paintings in Newlyn, to which he added £223 from his other commissions. This was a fabulous sum for a working man. Skilled workers would be lucky to earn £100 year and the unskilled would be happy to make half that.

Settling in Langley Newlyn in 1882, Langley found his life's work as 'the first figure painter to depict incidents in the life of the fisherfolk', as he himself asserted. Regarded as the pioneer of the Newlyn Art Colony, Langley's approach to his painting of working people was deeply affected by his own working-class upbringing and the influence of his mother. He was a social realist who believed that Labour was the source of all wealth. This political stance infused his work which reflected his concern for the persistent hardship faced by the poor. Highlighting the tragedies as much as the day-to-day life of working folk, Langley also stressed the importance of working-class women to their families.

At first Langley painted in watercolour but then began to use oil colour, leading to major works such as 'Never Morning Wore to Evening but some Heart did Break' (1894; Birmingham Museums and Art Gallery). This shows a weeping young woman at the quay side, who is comforted by an older woman. In 1895 Langley was awarded the accolade of the Uffizi Gallery in Florence requesting him to donate a self portrait to the gallery's Medici Collection of portraits of famous artists. Langley's first wife, Clara, died in 1895. He married again and died in Penzance in 1922.

Latimer Street, Attwood Green/Lee Bank

A.H. Bevan's manuscript on 'Birmingham Street Names' for the City Surveyors Department relates this street to Hugh Latimer, a Protestant clergyman and reformer who came to prominence during the reign of Henry VIII and became Bishop of Worcester. Later resigning his bishopric, Latimer was arrested during the reign of Queen Mary. Henry's oldest child by his first wife Catherine of Aragon, Mary was a devout Catholic and was determined to bring England back to the true religion, as she saw it. Latimer was arrested and though he was more than 80 years old, he was sentenced to be burnt at the stake for heresy along with another Protestant stalwart, Nicholas Ridley, Bishop of London and formerly Bishop of Rochester. He is commemorated in Ridley Street, which lies on the other side of Bath Row and goes along the ruins of St Thomas's Church and between Washington Street and Granville Street.

On 16 October 16, 1555 Latimer and Ridley were taken from the Tower of London to their horrible deaths. Arriving at the scene of their martyrdom, they knelt before the pile of faggots and prayed. They were tied to the same stake with a chain around their waists, leaving their hands and arms free. A sympathetic onlooker tied bags of gun powder about their necks to help speed their deaths. The faggots that were piled were lit. Latimer uttered words that have been immortalised: 'Be of good

A child playing in a yard in Latimer Street in the early 1960s. notice the miskins (dustbins), palings in front of the one house and the clean line of washing.

comfort, master Ridley, and play the man: we shall this day light such a candle, by God's grace, in England, as I trust shall never be put out'.

The flames were fast to reach the gunpowder tied about Latimer's neck and he died quickly, unlike Ridley whose death was agonising. The faggots of wood were wet and burned only around his legs which were completely burned. Taking pity on his terrible suffering, another onlooker pulled away some of the higher faggots to allow the flames to rise higher and explode the gunpowder so as to kill him.

Laurel Road, Handsworth

Going from Rookery Road to Antrobus Road this was named **Jawbone Lane** until 1879. It is a wonderfully descriptive name – but why was it so called?

Lawden Road, Bordesley

Going between Sandy Lane and Bolton Road, Lawden Road has fallen below the Small Heath Highway. It is believed that it was named after an owner of land.

Lawley Street, Duddeston

Named Lower Lawley Street until 1879, this follows the line of an ancient road that connected Watery Lane with Duddeston via a ford and later a bridge (see Lichfield Road and Moseley Road). It would seem to be named after Sir Robert Lawley of Canwell Hall near Tamworth. The fifth baronet Wenlock, his family had owned wide lands in Shropshire since 1471, and his wife, Jane Thompson, was heiress to estates in Yorkshire. He also owned property in Birmingham and Handsworth and was one of two MPs for

The LMS Goods Station in Lawley Street after a terrible fire in 1937.

Warwickshire in the late eighteenth and early nineteenth centuries. Before 1832, Birmingham was not represented in Parliament, but traditionally one of Warwickshire's MPs was seen as 'looking' after Birmingham's interests. Lawley was that man. He was also an active supporter of the General Hospital and other local charities.

Lease Lane, City

A short street running from Bell Street to Edgbaston Street in the markets district of Birmingham, it disappeared in the redevelopment of the early 1960s. According to Joe McKenna it would seem to have been Lea's Lane and was named after Edward Lea, a wool draper in the 1600s.

Lea House Road, Stirchley

Going between Maryvale Road and Bournville Lane, and running parallel with the Pershore Road, Lea House Road is one of the few local street names tied into local history. Across Bournville Lane, **Bond Street**, **Regent Street** and **Oxford Street** all are reminiscent of the major shopping streets in London, but Lea House Road recalls Lea House Farm – as does nearby **Lea Yield Close**, off Sparrey Drive.

Ledsam Street, Ladywood

When I was a youngster all Brummies knew the importance of the Welsh to Birmingham. We took our water from the Elan Valley in Radnorshire and were grateful for that, proudly proclaiming that it was the best water in the world – and it is; whilst hundreds of Welsh men and women taught in our schools, influencing generations of Brummies. Our Nan and Our Mom benefited from the strong teaching and musical love of 'old' Mr Lewis at Saint Mary's, Aston Cross; and in my own case I was privileged to have Cedric Gough as a teacher, a man who went on to become an inspirational headmaster of Saint George's, Hockley.

But the significance of the Welsh locally goes back much further than the twentieth century and in understanding that longstanding impact we are drawn into the origins of Birmingham. Until the conquest of the west midlands by the Angles in the sixth and seventh centuries, this land was occupied by Britons – the ancestors of the Welsh. Over the next two or three hundred years their language died out here but they did leave behind place names like Barr, meaning hill top, and Tame, signifying perhaps a dark river.

Then from at least the 1200s, drovers from Brecon and Radnorshire fetched their cattle from their uplands down across the Severn to sell in Wolverhampton, Walsall and Birmingham – where there was a Welsh Cross for this purpose at the top end of High Street, close to Bull Street. The Holders of Yardley and other provided pastures so that these cattle could be fattened up.

It is likely that the Welsh began to settle in Birmingham from the later Middle Ages and some of them became major figures in our history. In 1698 Sampson Lloyd the elder left Dolobran in Montgomeryshire because he and his family were persecuted for their Quaker faith. They became ironfounders in Birmingham and went on to join John Taylor the Brummagem button king in starting Taylor and Lloyd's Bank in High Street in 1765. The Lloyds are recalled in Dolobran Road, Montgomery Street and Sampson Road in Sparkbrook (see Sampson Road).

The Kenricks also made their mark. Archibald was the fourth son of a prominent Denbighshire family from Wynn Hall in Ruabon – perhaps leading to Wynn Street – and came to Birmingham about 1780. Soon after, he set up as a cast iron manufacturer in West Bromwich, so beginning one of the earliest and most important firms in that town. However, his descendants continued to play an active role in Birmingham. William Kenrick was mayor of Birmingham in 1877-8; and Sir George Hamilton Kenrick was Lord Mayor 32 years later – as was Wilfred Byng Kenrick in 1928-9. He was an acknowledged expert on education who was remembered in Byng Kenrick School.

Although the Kenricks intermarried with the Chamberlains and other Unitarian families, they seem to have had no connection with the wealthiest family of Welsh descent in Birmingham – the Goughs. Lords of the manor of Perry Barr and Edgbaston, they are known today as the Gough Calthorpes and are brought to mind in a host of places, including Gough Street behind the Mailbox.

In culture as much as in business the Welsh were influential. Edward Burne-Jones, the celebrated stained glass artist whose wonderful work enhances our wonderful churches St. Philip's and St Martin's, had Welsh ancestors – as did John Henry Langford. A self-taught working man, Langford strove to improve himself and the working class in general. Collaring as a chairmaker from when he was ten, he went on to teach himself mathematics, English grammar, Latin, French, and German

Pearce Brothers draper's and house furnisher's on the corner of Monument Road and Ledsam Street. Part of the Ledsam Works of Bellis and Morcom is visible on the right.

After his marriage, he lived in a back house in Bradford Street with his wife, Anne. Sadly she died of consumption and Langford also lost two of his four children. Persevering and dogged, Langford continued to write poetry and to teach evening classes to other working men and eventually he found work as a journalist. Best known today as a compiler of histories of Birmingham, Langford was indomitable of spirit and ever optimistic about humanity. He died in Fernley Road, Sparkhill in 1903.

Langford knew what it was to suffer hard times, as did many of the Welsh in Birmingham. In 1824 the realisation that there were 'very considerable number of poor persons connected with the Principality of Wales resident in the town and the neighbourhood' led a number of gentlemen to start a Saint David's Society. The Society's first report explained that 'on the most respectable authority, there are no less than between five and seven thousand Welsh families residing within fourteen miles of Birmingham, most of whom consist of the labouring class, far removed from their native land, subjected to a variety of difficulties and deprivations, and not entitled to parochial settlement in England'.

The driving force for the Society was Clement Ingleby, a leading solicitor who was associated with the setting up of the Fever Hospital in 1824. He is certainly remembered in **Ingleby Street**, Spring Hill but also probably in **Clement Street**, Ladywood. Although hailing from Cheadle, Ingleby and the other gentlemen who joined him on the Society's committee had a bond with Wales through 'descent, birth, relationship, property or race'. They included Thomas Eyre Lee, who may be recollected in **Eyre Street**, close to Ingleby Street in Spring Hill; and John Morton Ledsam and J.F. Ledsam.

The Ledsams were a noted family. Brought to mind in Ledsam Street (Ryland Street North until 1882) Ladywood, Martin Robson Smith tells me that in 1835 Joseph Frederick Ledsam (1791-1862) bought the Lordship of Northfield and some of the manorial land after the bankruptcy of the previous owner Joseph Weatherby Phipson. Martin states that this is the correct date and not the oft-quoted one of 1809, as is proven by Susan Tungate in her 1999 assignment entitled 'The Transfer of the Demesne Land and the Lordship of the Manor of Northfield and Weoley'. J. F. Ledsam's diary also contains the following relevant entry regarding the purchase: 'May 12, Bought Northfield Manor and Estates for £27,000 and 16th Weoley Castle for £9,000 inclusive of Timber, railway, etc.'

Furthermore according to Martin, "the Lordship that J. F. Ledsam bought was that of the Manor of Northfield and Weoley, whilst I understand the Lordship of Selly was subordinate to this and that the former did not actually 'include' the latter. Therefore the Ledsams, as I understand it, were not in fact the Lords of Selly. According to the Victoria County History for Worcestershire, the Lordship of Selly was last recorded as being held by the Gower family of Colmers in Kings Norton."

Joseph Ledsam himself had been high bailiff of Birmingham in 1812 and went on to be Deputy Lord Lieutenant of Warwickshire and High Sheriff of Worcestershire. An active supporter of the General Hospital through his chairmanships of the town's fundraising music festivals he was involved in many commercial undertakings – from the Birmingham Banking Company to the London and North Western Railway Company. He died in 1862. As for John Ledsam, he was a surgeon whilst a Daniel Ledsam was a plated metal manufacturer who owned Greet Mill and lived on Summer Hill – perhaps leading to the association of the nearby Ledsam Street with his family.

Regarding the Ledsams living at Weoley Park Farm, as far as Martin can tell only one member of the family ever lived there. This was James Goddington Ledsam (1836-1929), who for a time appears to have 'acted' as the Lord of the Manor, together with William Richard Hughes (Birmingham's Borough Treasurer), on behalf of the children of Joseph Ledsam (1823-1885) following his death; Joseph Ledsam had inherited the Lordship from his father Joseph Frederick Ledsam (1791-1862). James Goddington Ledsam was the youngest child of Joseph Frederick Ledsam and a brother to Joseph Ledsam. He inherited the Weoley Park Farm estate upon his father's death in 1862, and lived at the house at Weoley Park from around 1890 until 1903, later moving to another house on his land called 'Shendley' where he died on 14 January 1929. In addition, James had also inherited the Weoley Castle estate following the death of his other brother Frederick George Ledsam (1826-1876); incidentally Frederick Road in Selly Oak may be named after Frederick George but Martin needs to look into this further to be sure.

For all the wide ranging and positive effects the Welsh have had on our city, one more than most stands out – our Town Hall. In 1832 skilled Welshman were brought in to face the impressive new building with Anglesey marble. Sadly two of them died and are buried in St. Philip's Churchyard. Did this lead to the naming of **Anglesey Street** in Lozells? Today there are less Welsh in Birmingham than in the past but through the singing of the Canoldir Male Voice Choir and their chapels they maintain their strong and distinctive presence.

Lea Village, Lea Hall

What's the difference between Lea Hall, Kitts Green and Lea Village? The answer, there is no difference except in their names. Located in east Birmingham between Yardley and Sheldon and lying to the south and west of the River Cole, some people might say that Kitts Green lies to the north of the original London to Birmingham railway line and is cut through by Kitts Green Road itself. Starting from the end of Audley Road at Church Road in Yardley, Kitts Green Road stretches eastwards to the junction of the Meadway and East Meadway and is cut across in a north-south line by Lea Village the road.

If that is the case, then Lea Hall is to be found to the south of the railway tracks, Lea Hall Station and Lea Hall Road and is focused upon The Lea. But for most people, Kitts Green, Lea Hall and Lea Village are all the same area – although I stand to be corrected on that point.

Taking its name from the Old English word 'leah' meaning a woodland clearing, Lea or Lee was one of the first hamlets to be settled from the mother village of Yardley in the later Middle Ages. Probably a venture by a number of families, Lea

Village was mentioned first in 1275 and was connected to Yardley and Sheldon by a way that is now followed by the modern Lea Hall Road. The settlement itself was surrounded by perhaps four great open fields. These were divided into strips by the local agricultural folk and were cultivated in rotation so that one field lay fallow each year and could regain its goodness.

Lea was only a small hamlet, and its population would have been numbered in scores rather than hundreds. Amongst the early families associated with the settlement were the de la Lees, whose name meant of the Lee and who would have taken their name from the locality; the atte Wodes, signifying at the wood and who may have been called after a local wooded area; and the Otheyns.

As for Kittes Greene, thus **Kitts Green Road**, it is first mentioned in 1495 and it is likely that it was a green location, hence good land for farming, which was owned probably by a family called Kitte. According to Victor Skipp, the authority on the history of Yardley and Sheldon, Kitts Green was to found just to the east of the large building later known as Lea Hall, hence **Lea Hall Road**.

For centuries, Lea Hall and Kitts Green remained a secluded rural spot in the parish of Yardley in the County of Worcester. This is made clear as late as 1914 on the Ordnance Survey Map, upon which Kitts Green is shown as a hamlet that straggled up from Lea Hall, the big house, along the modern Lea Village that was known then as Lea Hall Road, up past the 'Lea Tavern' and along towards today's Yockleton Road. The only other building locally was The Lea. This was across the railway line, by the meeting of the modern Meadway, Green Lane and Outmoor Road.

The remoteness of Lea Hall was made plain for all Brummies one day late in November 1932, when a reporter from the *Evening Mail*, trekked out to Lea Village. It was such a jaunt to get there that the intrepid journalist declared that another name for the village 'would be World's End. It is at the Back of Beyond, round the lanes and far away. It might be a hundred miles from Birmingham. Actually it is within the city boundary. It is probably the loneliest, most rural and least known spot in Birmingham.'

The visit by the *Mail* man was prompted by a letter from one of the villagers who complained that Lea was one and half miles from train, tram, bus, post office, public telephone, doctor or police station. The villager pleaded that if the letter 'should catch the eye of some of our city councillors, they might inquire where Lea Village is'. Making his way to Lea Village, the Stanley of the Mail got lost in a maze of lanes beyond old Yardley, lanes that were twisted cunningly, full of mud and obscurity. Eventually, he spied a sign for Lea Hall and when he arrived at his destination he found a surprisingly fine, modern inn. The big house itself, which gave its name to Lea Hall, was 'a mournful spectacle. It is one of several Elizabethan houses in this part of Warwickshire on which decay is laying a heavy hand'. Its ancient walls were covered with ivy, which was also growing in through the windows.

Although, part of Brum since Yardley had been incorporated within the City in 1911, Lea Hall was remote and forgotten – although it was felt that 'in due course, therefore, it may lose some of its present isolation.' The loss of that isolation came much sooner than the reporter could have envisaged. Desperate for land on which to build better quality homes for so many of its working-class and lower middle-class citizens, Birmingham Council took control of the land in and about Lea Hall and Kitts Green.

From 1936 a huge estate was developed of 3,486 municipal houses – the third biggest in the City. Indeed the 50,000th council house built in Birmingham since 1919 was at Fellmeadow Road, Lea Hall. The district that was urbanised stretched from the Glebe Farm Estate in the west to Gossey Lane in the east and had Kitts Green Road as its northern limit. To the south it reached Poole Lane (The Meadway). After the Second World War a further 3,732 homes were constructed by the corporation on another 460 acres of the Lea Hall Estate. Thousands of people from Duddeston, Ashted, Nechells, Vauxhall, Aston and Summer Lane were moved into good quality homes and today their grandchildren live in a populous and integral part of Brum – a far cry from the village at the back of beyond.

Leach Heath Road, Rubery

Going from Whetty Lane to **Leach Green Lane**, this recalls a heath on the edge of Birmingham that was named after a family called Leach.

Lee Bank Middleway, Attwood Green/Lee Bank

Because it had no name of its own for so long, the Lee Bank neighbourhood has suffered from inattention. Always part of the manor of Birmingham, it has sometimes been seen incorrectly as part of Edgbaston. Even the post-war planners were unsure as to what to call the district. At first it was scheduled under Bath Row, and eventually it was named Lee Bank after one of its roads, itself recalling a solicitor named Lee who owned the land upon which the fine Georgian houses in Lee Crescent were built. Lee Crescent overlooked Lee Bank Road, now Lee Bank Middleway. Bank, meanwhile, is the West Midland word for a hill – a bank. Having emerged in the nineteenth century and been cleared and refashioned in the mid-twentieth century, Lee Bank is once more in the throes of change and has now been called Attwood Green.

Throughout the eighteenth and nineteenth centuries, Lee Bank was known as Holloway Head (see Holloway Head). South of that road, gardens were laid out in 1764, but within fourteen years Windmill Street and Bow Street were apparent on Hanson's Map – and buildings were also obvious along Brick Kiln Lane (later the Horsefair). In 1781, the map maker drew another plan of the town and showed the windmill itself, standing close to where Florence Street would be cut. Further development was slow, and the district remained an attractive one outside Birmingham. Indeed, in 1813 an advertisement offered the lease of a pleasant house with a good garden, orchard and soft water near to the Windmill, Exeter Row.

By the late 1830s, the winding Bellbarn Road had come into view as had Ryland Road and Spring Street. A new road to Smithfield Market was also shown on Bradshaw's map of 1840. Running from Islington Row, its bottom end led across

Little Bow Street in the 1920s. This was the only street in Birmingham with no through way. It came off Bow Street, itself connecting Windmill Street and Irving Street. The steps in the background of the photo led to the Horsefair. I have no evidence to explain the origin of Bow Street.

Bristol Street to Bromsgrove Street and hence to Smithfield Market. This un-named became Great Colmore Street, after the Colmores who owned the district. Within a decade it had offshoots such as Cregoe Street, recalling the family which inherited the property of the Colmores.

Like nearby Ladywood, the Holloway Head neighbourhood was filled with back-to-backs and like each working-class district of Brum, it was packed with hard-collaring folk. Their homes were knocked down after the Second World War and high-rise flats and maisonettes arose in their place. Today, new developments are once again changing Lee Bank and many of its folk have been moved out.

Leek Street, City

Leek Street was a short street that went from Coleshill Street to the meeting of Jennens Row and Buck Street, across the way from which was Bartholomew Street. Leek Street and Buck Street were among a number of little streets in this locality. Another was Doe Street and like Buck Street it seems to have been named by someone keen on deer. Half way down Leek Street was then even smaller Drury Lane, which would appear to have taken its name from the street in London. Leek Street is shown on Bradford's map of 1750. It disappeared in the redevelopment of the 1960s. There is no intimation as to why it was so called.

Lench Street, Gun Quarter

A tiny street that is all but blocked out by St Chad's Queensway and the dual carriageway of Lancaster Street, Lench Street runs off Vesey Street, which itself comes off Loveday Street. It recalls a William Lench, who apparently was the heir of a William Goldsmythe. By a deed dated 11 March 1526, Lench placed various properties in Birmingham and the immediate neighbourhood in the hands of feoffees (trustees in effect) and ordered that the rents and profits of the premises should be applied 'for the repairing the ruinous ways and bridges in and about the said town of Birmingham, where it should want, and for default of such uses should bestow the rents and profits of the premises to the poor living within the said town, where there should be most need, according to the appointment and disposition of the said feoffees for the time being, or to the major part of them, or to other pious uses, according to the like discretion and appointment.'

No other information is available about William Lench, but in the succeeding generations Lench's Trust drew to it smaller trusts and received the land and monies from other benefactors. As such it began to make its mark. With its funds, the Trust built the first of its almshouses in Digbeth. It stood until 1765. In the late seventeenth or eighteenth centuries, the trustees then had built a second block of almshouses on the outskirts of the town upon a croft (field) near Walmer Lane (now Lancaster Street) and at the bottom of Steelhouse Lane. Toulmin Smith, the indefatigable researcher into Birmingham's early history, asserted that:

from their doors or windows, the inmates could enjoy one of the fairest prospects of which our delightful county could boast, even in those early days, when black, smoking chimneys were fewer, and the limits of the domain of brick and mortar much more confined than nowadays. Away on the left could be seen in the distance the gently rising eminence of Barr-beacon, and the pleasant hill on which Oscott College now stands. Nearer, and rather more to the right, would be seen the minaret-crowned towers of Aston Hall, and the tall, graceful spire of the pretty village church, rising from the midst of a grove of trees; still further to the right, (almost in the middle of the prospect) the village of Erdington, crowning the little eminence called Gravelly Hill, and behind it the well-wooded park of Sutton Coldfield; and away to the right might then be seen the beautiful spire of Coleshill Church. This almshouse was indeed a pleasant harbour of refuge for the aged poor, weary and worn with the battle of life, where they might end their days in peaceful retirement, away from the busy hive in which they had toiled during their earlier years. But the town grew, and ere long surrounded the little group of almshouses; the furnaces of Kettle's steel-houses sent forth smoke to cloud the prospect, and, by and by, rows of houses sprang up in Walmer Lane to block it out altogether.

Westley's Map of 1731, the first map of Birmingham, shows this group of Alms House lying amidst fields. Lench Street recalls them. In his book *Old and New Birmingham* (1880) Robert K Dent declared that 'the Charities of Lench and others, commonly called Lench's Trust, stand first among the Birmingham charities, being both the most ancient, and at the present time the most actively useful'. It continues to do good work; its older alms house by the Children's Hospital at Five Ways have been sold and now it has more modern accommodation in Moseley Village.

Ley Hill Farm Road, Northfield

This runs opposite Ley Hill Recreation Ground and Ley Hill Hall, now demolished and the former home of Christian Kunzle, the Swiss cake maker and the philanthropist. Ley comes from the Anglo-Saxon word leah, meaning a clearing – and the hill is still obvious. Ley Hill Farm was mentioned in 1344-1445, and a man called atte Leye was noted in the Subsidy Roll of 1275. In the mid-twentieth century, Ley Hill Farm became the recreation ground and the land across the way was mostly developed as a council estate. Recently, this itself has been cleared and replaced by better quality housing.

Lichfield Road, Aston

Peter de Bermingham was the Lord of a manor that was not worth a lot. There was farmland in the eastern part of his estate, but in the west in what is now Ladywood, Brookfields, Winson Green, Spring Hill and Rotton Park the land was mostly was heath or wooded. As such it did not give Peter much of an income. It seems, however, that Peter was a keen observer of changing times. He realised that there was a growing population locally and that those people were shifting away from bartering to a cash economy. Moreover many of them were small-scale farmers who were also making small metal goods such as nails, bits for horses and the like and they needed somewhere to sell their wares.

Alert to these socio-economic imperatives, Peter literally spotted a gap in the market – and filled it. In 1166 he obtained a royal charter to hold a weekly market at his 'castle', ensuring that Birmingham would become the local centre for the selling and buying of things rather than Aston, Yardley, Halesowen, Harborne and elsewhere. His 'castle' was hard on the eastern boundary of his manor, on the slopes leading down to the River Rea from the red sandstone ridge on which the Council House now stands. Importantly this castle was not only amidst the better cultivated part of the manor but also it controlled a crossing point of the Rea – one which was significant for a number of routes.

A cracking shot of the Lichfield Road, Aston in the later 1950s shortly before these shops were to be chucked into the miskin of history. Many of us will remember that one shop owner defiantly resisted clearance and continued trading as a lone symbol of a once thriving Aston Cross – that was the famed Thompson's the pork butcher's. That shop is between the two lorries, close to the greengrocery display of William French on the footpath. In the background is Ansell's Brewery and the HP Sauce factory.

Amongst them was the road from Wolverhampton. It went via West Bromwich and Handsworth (along the modern Soho Road), down what is now Great Hampton Street, up Constitution Hill and old Snow Hill to Dale End. Thence it headed into High Street and Digbeth and to the crossing point of the Rea where Deritend Bridge would later be built.

Similarly the road from Dudley, the seat of the overlord of Peter de Bermingham, came by way of Smethwick and along the modern Dudley Road, Spring Hill, Summer Hill, Sand Pits, Parade, Pinfold Street, and Dudley Street to Edgbaston Street –whence it also went on to Digbeth. The Halesowen road also reached Digbeth through Edgbaston Street, arriving there via today's Hagley Road, Islington Row, Bath Row, Holloway Head and Smallbrook Street.

By contrast, the Alcester Road probably came across Camp Hill and down Watery Lane to another crossing point of the Rea, at what is now Lawley Street, on the borders of the manors of Duddeston and Bordesley. It is likely that the original route from Coventry also came through this ford. However, the rapid growth of Birmingham led to a realignment of both roads so as to cross the Rea at Deritend Bridge and thus go through the burgeoning market town.

That rearrangement of the Coventry Road is plain to see today. As it comes down past Greenway Street it makes a sharp turn to the south west, bringing it into line with Cattell Road. If the road continued without this alteration then it would go by Kingston Hill Recreation Ground and Itychcoo Park (Garrison Lane Rec) to the junctions of Watery Lane, Lower Dartmouth Street and Lawley Street.

All these routes generally approached Birmingham in a south-east /north-west axis, because of the lie of the Rea crossings; but there were two major routes to Lichfield (and Tamworth) which went in a south west/north east direction. Yet although they may not have gone across the Rea, crucially they were connected with the roads that did so.

The first route came from Worcester and part of it was later known as the Bristol Road. It went along the Roman road of Icknield Street to Droitwich and thence through Edgbaston to join with the Halesowen Road and thus come into Birmingham. Thence it passed down High Street, Dale End, Coleshill Street, Prospect Row and Ashted Row to Bloomsbury Street where it went up to Nechells Green and down Thimblemill Lane to join the second road to Lichfield. Letters patent were dated at Birmingham in 1235 when the king was travelling from Lichfield to Worcester.

Birmingham's archaeologist, Mike Hodder, and Steven Bassett are the historians who have done most to draw back the heavy cloak that shrouds Birmingham from view in the Anglo-Saxon period. Bassett believes that the convoluted route of the road from Worcester to Lichfield contrasts with 'the gently sinuous courses of the area's other through routes' and therefore proposes that in medieval times the premier road from Worcester to Lichfield that came through the manor of Birmingham may have still gone along the Icknield Street.

Be that as it may, there was another main route to Lichfield, along part of which the modern Lichfield Road in Aston lies. This was the second significant south west/north east road in the manor of Birmingham and it came from Harborne. As Bassett emphasises, this was a valuable possession of the Church of Lichfield and it also had an importance locally. The churches of Edgbaston and Handsworth had originated as chapels of Harborne, whilst West Bromwich and perhaps Selly and Birmingham had once been part of Harborne parish. In these circumstances, any road linking Harborne with Lichfield would be longstanding and significant.

This route came through the modern Vivian Road, part of Harborne High Street, Harborne Road, Broad Street, Colmore Row and Steelhouse Lane to Aston Street and Gosta Green. From there it went along Aston Road where it crossed the Aston Brook (also called the Hockley Brook) and passed down the Aston Road North and the Lichfield Road itself, which begins at Aston Cross. Notably from Broad Street to Steelhouse Lane the road ran partly along the red sandstone ridge which stretches from Northfield to Sutton Coldfield and upon which the centre of Birmingham is built.

This Harborne to Lichfield Road crossed the Wolverhampton Road at Snow Hill, whereby travellers could easily head off along Bull Street into High Street and the town of Birmingham; whilst at Gosta Green it connected with the old line of the Coventry Road via what was to become Woodcock Street and Belmont Row – which then went into Lawley Street and hence to Watery Lane.

Through this latter route the Harborne to Lichfield Road also came into contact with the Worcester to Lichfield Road. However, the two of them finally came together when Thimblemill Lane joined what is now the Lichfield Road. Thus united, the Lichfield Road crossed the Tame by Salford Bridge, which itself was in existence by 1290. From there it may have gone either through Erdington and Sutton Coldfield, where a highway was mentioned in 1176, or through Perry and a bridge across the Tame.

However, there was no bridge over the Aston Brook. In his *History of Birmingham*, William Hutton despaired that 'one mile from Birmingham, upon the Lichfield road, which is sixteen miles, to the disgrace of the community, was a river without a bridge till 1792'. By this date there was also a **Lichfield Street** in the expanding town of Birmingham. It led from Old Square to Aston Street and is shown Westley's Map of Birmingham in 1731. Cut out on the estate that was owned by the wealthy Quaker, John Pemberton, it was part of a development aimed at the wealthier of Birmingham's citizens. However, as Edgbaston gained in prestige and popularity from the 1820s, so the Lichfield Street neighbourhood declined in status. By the middle years of the nineteenth century it was regarded as one of the poorest parts of Birmingham and was then cleared under the Corporation Street Improvement Scheme. Its line is now followed by that part of Corporation Street that goes from Old Square to Steelhouse Lane.

As for the Lichfield Road this was not turnpiked until 1807. Administered by trusts authorised by private acts of Parliament, turnpikes took their name from a pike that formed a barrier to traffic and that was turned to allow access. These turnpike trusts were empowered to levy tolls on travellers. The money raised was spent on the upkeep and maintenance of the route. This involved the digging of drainage ditches and laying down a surface of stones and cinders.

In 1840 it was reported that the Lichfield Road was in a poor condition and had been adversely affected both by the competition of the railways and by the abolition of statute labour – unpaid labour on public projects that was obligatory under law. Thirty-two years later the trust was abolished. By this time Aston was developing rapidly and a bustling shopping thoroughfare emerged that stretched along the Aston Road North, Aston Cross and much of the Lichfield Road. The destruction of old Aston annihilated this wonderful shopping road. Today the Lichfield Road remains a major through route, although much traffic now bypasses it on the A38 M.

Lickey Road, Rednal

Striking upwards from the Bristol Road at the old Longbridge Works, Lickey Road was the entrance to a world of make-believe for hundreds of thousands of Brummie children. Catching the tram from Navigation Street, they would alight at the terminal by Green Lane and then head off into the Lickey Hills for a day out in the country that was their holiday. Fortified by bottles of cold tea and jam sandwiches wrapped up in the Birmingham mail, they would be looked after by Our Wench, their older sister – unless, of course, it was a Sunday and mom and dad had come out with them as well.

They followed in the steps of ancient peoples, for a flint arrow head and a flint scraping tool from the Neolithic period (New Stone Age) have been found on Rednal Hill. After the Norman invasion, the Lickeys were part of the royal Manor of Bromsgrove and were a royal hunting ground. The area was with deer and the Normans introduced rabbits that were kept in large enclosures known as warrens, hence **Warren Lane**. In 1682, Bromsgrove was sold by the crown to the Earl of Plymouth, whose descendants owned the Lickeys for the next 250 years.

In the late nineteenth century the coming of the railway and a station encouraged housing development around Barnt Green and there were concerns that the Lickeys would be lost. Consequently, in 1888 the Birmingham Society for the Preservation of Open Spaces purchased Rednal Hill and handed to the City in trust. They also arranged for Pinfield Wood and Bilberry Hill to be leased on a peppercorn (nominal) rent. The City went on to buy Cofton Hill, Lickey Warren and Pinfield Wood in 1920, followed three years later by the purchase of the Rose Hill Estate from the Cadbury. All across the Lickeys there was now free public access. The Lickey Hills were designated a Country Park in 1971 and the Visitor Centre was completed in 1990.

In 1904, J. R. R. Tolkien moved with his brother and mother, Mabel, to Fern Cottage in the grounds of Oratory House, Mabel was ill with diabetes and it was felt that the fresh air of the Lickeys would be good for her. The hills were a magical place for the young Tolkien, with the smoke of Birmingham to the north east and the green of Worcestershire and the Malvern Hills to the south west. Many people feel resonances between the Lickeys and the Shire, the land of the Hobbits, in both *The Hobbit* and the *Lord of the Rings* – and certainly the Lickeys had an ancient feel.

The Bilberry Hill Tea Rooms at the Lickey Hills.

In his history of Kings Norton and Northfield Wards, Arthur B. Lock asserted that the word Lickey was of Celtic origin and meant a flat stone. This seems unlikely. Between 1255 and 1408 various documents record la Lec, Lekheye, Lekhaye, Lykeheye and Lickhay. All contain the French definite article 'le' meaning the, and it is probable that 'le' went before hale. This was derived from the Anglo-Saxon word gehaeg meaning enclosure – in this case a forest enclosure. However a small brook runs through the hills and the Anglo-Saxon word for a stream was 'lece', hence perhaps Lickey.

Lifford Lane, Kings Norton

Linking Broad Lane and the Pershore Road at Cotteridge, Lifford Lane is an enchanting spot. Despite the industrial buildings hereabouts it still has a rural charm. The location of one the City's Household Recycling Centres, it is also the site of a reservoir that is a favourite fishing place for anglers. In fact, the 'rezzer' and its surroundings are a wonderful example of Birmingham's greenness, lying as they do at the junction of the Stratford upon Avon and the Worcester Canal and by the River Rea Cycle Route.

Vivian Bird felt that the name came from Lifford Hall, itself relating to James Hewitt Lord Chancellor of Ireland and Viscount Lifford of Lifford Donegal. This is not the case. In 1275, the Subsidy Rolls for sub Norton mention an Adam de la (of the) Ford and the name Lifford would seem to have come from a ford on the River Rea. The most longstanding building locally is Lifford Hall. It has been the centre of local folklore, with stories abounding that tunnels ran from there Lifford to Kings Norton Church a mile away. Tunnels were indeed found in the archaeological excavations that took place in the mid-1990s but they were underground mill leats (water trenches). This was because part of Lifford Hall was a watermill, which may date from the fourteenth century.

In the Boulton and Watt Archive is a parchment dated 1 December 1785 which mentions Thomas Dobbs Lifford Rolling Mills at Kings Norton. In 1838 a second mill was built away from the house. These Adderley Park Mills were founded by Thomas Bayliss & Son and became the Kings Norton Metal Co. It was a rolling mill that produced brass, copper and other metal alloy strip. The Royal Mint became a customer and a minting plant is reputed to have been installed in 1914. Pennies were minted there in 1918 and 1919 with the Kings Norton mark. In the 1930 the plant moved to Witton and the site was bought by Slough Estates. It became the Birmingham Factory Centre and is now the Kings Norton Business Centre. Nearby and also off Lifford Lane was the paper of James Baldwin (see Baldwin Road).

In the early 1800s, Lifford Hall was given a crenellated wall and an octagonal turret was also built. No longer did it look like a mill, instead it seemed to be a grand Gothic structure, which gave rise to legends of a Saxon chapel or monastic establishment at Lifford. In fact the Hall itself is basically a seventeenth century Jacobean house.

The reservoir was built by the Worcester Canal Company in the 1790s as a means to placate the local mill owners who feared that the canal would leave them with too little water to power their mills. Lifford Lane is also noticeable for its Guillotine Gates. These are vertical lock gates built at the end of the eighteenth century between the Stratford Canal and the Worcester Canals. They were devised to stop water flowing from the canal of each company, regardless of which side was higher, and symbolise the intense competition rivalry between canal companies and their concern to conserve their own water supplies. The existing gates probably date to the nineteenth century, although the lock arrangement may have been in place since this part of the canal was opened in 1796. Each lock consists of a brick-lined stone-dressed stop lock with a cast iron guillotine gate framework which is thought to be unique. They were in use until 1943.

Engineers on the Worcester and Birmingham Canal faced other major difficulties. They had to construct a flight of 30 locks by Tardebigge to get the canal up to the Birmingham plateau, and also a 1½ mile long tunnel in Kings Norton, after which is named **Tunnel Road** off Lifford Lane.

Lindsworth Road, Kings Norton

Looping round from Broad Meadow Lane to **Lindsworth Approach** and Monyhull Road, this is an ancient name first mentioned in a twelfth century document that included references relating to about the year 705. Noted as Lindesworde in the Domesday Book of 1086, it means the enclosure (worth) by the lime trees (lind). Lindsworth Farm was developed after the Second World War.

Little Bromwich Road, Little Bromwich

Going between Bordesley Green East and Yardley Green Road and hemmed in between the old fever hospital and Hey Barnes Recreation Ground, Little Bromwich Road calls out of a district name that has all but fallen out of use in modern Birmingham. As part of the parish of Aston, Little Bromwich is first mentioned in the 1200s when Henry Russel of Little Bromwich made a grant of tenements and lands to John son of William at Grove of Erdington. It seems likely that the name 'Little' was added to differentiate the place from the adjoining Bromwich, which was distinguished with the prefix of Castle. Bromwich itself means the dwelling or farm where broom grows.

From the later Middle Ages, there seemed to be two manors of Little Bromwich: one was also known as Alum Rock and covered the Alum Rock and Treaford Hall estates, hence Treaford Lane; the other was also called Ward End and consisted of the Ward End Hall Estate. According to John Tomlinson's Survey of 1759, both sections were actually part of one manor. Still, as Alum Rock and Ward End emerged as distinct districts in the late nineteenth and early twentieth centuries, then Little Bromwich came to be applied only to a small area. This was bounded by Little Bromwich Road in the east, Blake Lane in the west, Bordesley Green East in the north and Yardley Green Road in the south. Much of this land was taken up by the city's Fever Hospital (built on Howlett's Farm) and its presence may have led folk to drop the name Little Bromwich and adopt that of Bordesley Green. The rest of this shrunken Little Bromwich is the attractive estate of the Ideal Benefit Society (see Daniels Road). (See also Alum Rock Road and Ward End Road).

Livery Street, City

'With a face as long as Livery Street I walked up Colmore Row', so goes the line in Laurie Hornsby's song about the sayings of working-class Brum – and this one was reserved for people who were mardy or miserable. Their long faces were reminiscent of the great length of Livery Street, which stretched out from Colmore Row to Great Hampton Street. It is not indicated on Westley's Map of 1731, but is shown seventeen years later on Bradford's Map, A few buildings are clear at the top of Livery Street, but downwards from what would become Edmund Street (then Charles Street and Hill Street) there are merely the words 'land for building' – and below that area there are fields. The Map also includes a list of Birmingham's streets and figures for buildings and inhabitants in each of them: nothing is recorded for Livery Street. Hanson's Map of 1781 makes plain that Livery Street has developed as far down as Lionel Street, below which other streets have been laid out on the Newhall Estate (see Colmore Row.

Joe McKenna states that Livery Street was named after Swan's Riding Academy which stood on the corner of Cornwall Street (then called Bread Street), which is given credibility by a description in Drake's *Picture of Birmingham* in 1825, which reads:

Looking down Livery Street from what was then Monmouth Street, which became part of Colmore Row in 1879 after the Council House was built. This photo must have been taken before that date. The empty premises covered in posters bring to the fore the redevelopment that was then taking place on the Colmore Estate (see Colmore Row).

> we cross Livery Street, where, at a little distance, we perceive a lumbering mass of brick-work, originally designed for an Amphitheatre, for the exhibition of equestrian shows. It is now, like the two Theatres before mentioned, converted into a Dissenting Place of Worship.

Since the mid-nineteenth century, the north east side of Livery Street has been dominated by Snow Hill Station.

Livingstone Road, Birchfield

Stretching from the Birchfield Road to Putney Road, this Livingstone Road, like the one in Kings Heath, is named after the famous Scottish explorer. David Livingstone was a man of many parts for he was also a missionary, doctor, scientist and anti-slavery activist. He spent 30 years in Africa and explored almost a third of the continent, from its southern tip almost to the equator. Acclaimed as the first white man to see Victoria Falls, he never discovered the source of the Nile as he hoped. During the late 1860s he was not heard of for a number of years, prompting international concern. The New York Time sent out another explorer, Henry Stanley, to find Livingstone. He did so in 1871 on Lake Tanganyika and greeted Livingstone with the famous words, 'Dr. Livingstone, I presume'. Livingstone died a year later.

Lloyd Street, Small Heath

A short street between Golden Hillock Road and Wordsworth Road, Lloyd Street is named after James Lloyd, who owned Golden Hillock Farm in the early nineteenth century (see Golden Hillock Road).

Lodge Road, Hockley

In the Inclosure Awards for Birmingham Heath in 1802, this is given as Lodge and Winson Green Road; however it then became known as Hockley Pool Road until 1884 as it led towards Hockley Little Pool. Hockley Pool itself was, of course, so important to Matthew Boulton (see Boulton Road). Thenceforth it reverted to Lodge Road. The Plan of the Parish of Birmingham by John Snape in 1839 indicates a lodge above Hockley Little Pool on the expanse of land known as Birmingham Heath (see Heath Street). This had been the hunting ground of the lords of the manor of

A view along Lodge Road in the Edwardian period. The photo is dominated by children walking and playing in the horse road – notice the lad with the hoop on the right – and has a resonance with the late 1950s photo of Monument Road and Kings Edwards Road. Separated by half a century and by styles of clothing, the children in both shots are bonded by their same lifestyles and by the use of the street as a playground. On the right is Freeman Hardy and Willis, the second shop on the north side of Lodge Road as this wonderful shopping thoroughfare went from Icknield Street. The carter who is behind the lamppost is approaching the Baptists Chapel that lies back from the road. It is a busy scene, a far cry from the inactivity of the shortened Lodge Road.

Birmingham and the lodge originally would have been a house used by someone who watched over the estate. Later it was made into a fine building called Monument House and in which lived John Perrott from 1737(see Monument Road).

When Brookfields and that part of Hockley around Lodge Road were developed from the mid-1800s, the top end of Lodge Road became a superb shopping centre. Because it started at the bottom of Key Hill where the land levelled out this part of Lodge Road was called The Flat. It remained a vital shopping thoroughfare until the redevelopments of the 1960s. Now The Flat part of Lodge Road is a cul-de-sac that ends just before Hurdlow Avenue. It is s sad spot, bereft of its shopkeepers and shoppers. The rest of Lodge road now begins at Goode Street and still goes up to the coming together of the Handsworth New Road and the Winson Green Road.

Longbridge Lane, Longbridge

The long bridge at The Austin is no more. One of the most famous conveyor bridges in the land, until very recently it went across the main A38 Bristol Road South and linked the production lines at the West Works with those of the South Works. At one time 360,000 cars a year passed along the bridge and it remained in use until that fateful day in April 2005 when MG Rover collapsed, forcing thousands of car workers and those in the supply industry into unemployment. A massive 1,000 tonne crane lifted away the main section of the conveyor that weighed 500 tonnes and was 510 feet in length. One more landmark of the iconic Longbridge car factory disappeared and one more bond with the manufacturing history of our city was smashed.

Yet contrary to what many people think, this distinctive bridge did not give its name to Longbridge – for it was only constructed in 1972 at the time when production of the Allegro was beginning. Instead the origins of Longbridge lie firmly in the rural history of Northfield. A map compiled in 1894 under the directions of the Kings Norton Joint Committee clearly shows a place called Longbridge between what would become Longbridge Lane (which had been Hopwood Road) and the River Rea. It was just to the west of the Bristol and Birmingham Railway line and was located where the celebrated car factory would be built and it seems that there was indeed a long bridge over the watercourse. Moreover, records in the Middlemore family mention a Longbridge Farm in the late sixteenth century.

Longbridge was then deep in the countryside. A little to the north and back along the Bristol Road was Tessall Farm, brought to mind today in Tessall Lane; to the west and down the Bristol Road South was Colmer's Farm, near to the modern Clift Rock Road; to the south and off Lickey Road was Rednal House, later cleared for the cutting of Edgwood Road and others; and to the east was Little Hawkesley Farm and its moat, close to where Culmington Road would emerge, with Cofton Common further away.

Except for a few old clay pits, the land was overwhelmingly agricultural. Other farms included Low Hill Farm, recalled in **Low Hill Lane**, and Nimmings Farm, along Grovelly Lane and close to the modern Ilsham Grove. And not far from where

LONGBRIDGE NR. NORTHFIELD.

An early photograph of Longbridge, perhaps around the early 1920s. On the right are the South Works of The Austin, formerly the White and Pyke's tin box factory. The rural nature of the area is obvious, as the trees to the left stand in what would become the West Works. The omnibus is just passing Longbridge Lane on the right.

workers and reporters gathered during the Rover crisis at Q Gate, there was a mysterious house called the Wonders, about where CAB 1 (Car Assembly Building) would be built.

The Kings Norton Map does also show, however, a squareish building close to the Bristol Road South. Although it is un-named it was the newly-built works of the printers White and Pyke's. The premises were used for making tin boxes, but by about 1901 the ventured had closed and the factory remained empty until it was taken over four years later by Herbert Austin for the making of cars. Austin was a key figure in the fast-moving development of the British car industry. One of the great industrial figures of the twentieth century, he was born in Buckinghamshire but went to Australia at the age of sixteen. By the time he returned to Britain as an adult in 1893 he had become a key figure in the Wolseley Sheep Shearing company, the British operations of which were to be based at the Sydney Works in Alma Street, Aston.

Two years before, the Lanchester brothers had built in Birmingham the first British car which was four-wheeled and driven by petrol. Perhaps influenced by them, also in 1895 Austin made a two-horse power car with three wheels and a horizontal water-cooled system. After his work at the Wolseley had ended, he laboured tirelessly late into the night on producing horseless carriages, testing them on the road at weekends. Despite the many engineering problems, the long hours and the hard work, this was a thrilling time. Wherever Austin and other pioneers drove their cars there was exhilaration and an excitement amongst both designers and onlookers. Invigorated by car making, Austin had a vision of everybody driving cars. Unable to further that dream at the Wolseley, he decided to set up on his own.

With a far-sightedness that few recognised at the time, he bought the disused factory of White and Pyke's for £7,750. Seven miles outside Birmingham it was far into the Worcestershire countryside. Looking back from the perspective of 1954, Mr L.P. Appleton, then the secretary and manager of the Bournville Village Trust, remembered the district as a remote outpost. Fine trout were taken from the brook by the works and wild daffodils were picked in the fields between Austin's factory and Northfield Station.

Friends tried to discourage Austin from buying Longbridge, as it became known. They told him that mechanics would not travel so far to work, but he ignored them. The small factory had been purpose-built, it was close to road and rail links, and it had room for expansion. There was another pulling factor. Because Longbridge was in a rural spot, the air was clearer than in smoky Birmingham. This less polluted atmosphere was important because it helped to achieve a good paint finish for the slow drying coach enamels that were used then.

Compared to the £100,000 capital on which most motor concessions and agencies were run, Austin had just £15,000 – and even part of that had been put forward by the son of an old friend, Captain Frank Kayser. However, about a year afterwards, Harvey du Cross joined the firm. He was the managing director of the Swift Cycle Company and was the son of the chairman of Dunlop and his financial input was vital for the success of Austin's venture.

Amongst the employees taken on by Austin was Mr W. A. Howitt, his private secretary from the Wolseley. Howitt later explained that first and foremost, Austin was a worker who could do all types of work on a motor car and 'was not ashamed to take his coat off and demonstrate to a workman, who might seem a little confused, the right way to go'.

A grafter who was plain in his speech and dress, Austin was a talented engineer and designer whose mind soared to the possibilities of what might be. Like Boulton, Watt, Gillott and all the other heroes of the Birmingham workshop, his practicality was inspired by vision and on the wall of his office at Longbridge was displayed the belief that 'Most everything worthwhile is born of some dreamer's dream'. Austin's dream was to build cars at his own factory and see those cars driven on the road by a public that was able to afford motorised transport. He realised his dream.

By 1907, Longbridge had 400 workers who were able to build 147 cars by hand. Over the next seven years, the number of employees grew to 2,000 whilst annual output of various models extended to 983. During the First World War, the Austin (pronounced by Brummies as Orstin) was vital to the war effort and the workforce expanded vastly to 20,000. It was essential that some of these people lived close to the factory and so Austin bought 120 acres of land and built three large hostels and

50 brick houses. He also imported 200 wooden houses from the United States of America. These buildings can be seen still in Austin Village where many of the roads are named after trees. Amongst them are **Cedar Row**, **Maple Way**, **Rowan Way** and **Cypress Way**. The focal road of the village is the aptly-named **Central Avenue**.

After the First World War, a further development of mostly private houses led to the disappearance of nearby Tessall Farm, but it was not until the 1950s that Longbridge became a populous suburb. A municipal state was built on Hawkesley Farm and both the Council and private builders erected houses in Longbridge itself and in adjoining districts.

Longbridge grew because of Austin and his works. The district and the factory were inextricably tied together and were vital to Birmingham's prowess as a manufacturing city. It was from Longbridge in 1922 that came the Austin Seven, a phenomenally popular small car that opened up car ownership to the lower middle class – so much so that with a falling birth rate during the inter-war years the question was asked: 'What was more important to middle-class families: a baby or a baby Austin?' And it was also from Longbridge in 1959 that came out another feted car – the Mini. Designed by Alex Issigonis this vehicle made in Birmingham became one of the icons of the twentieth century.

With the mass production of cars now ended at Longbridge, the people of the factory and the area have had to adjust to a strange and difficult situation. They've been knocked down, but unlike the conveyor bridge that is down and out forever the Brummies of Longbridge will do what Brummies always do when they're knocked down: they'll pick theirselves up, dust theirselves down and take on the world again.

Lordswood Road, Harborne

Heading down from the Hagley Road to Harborne High Street, Lordswood Road recalls the local wood that was owned by the Lord of Harborne.

Louise Lorne Road, Moseley

A short street going between Trafalgar Road and the Moseley Road, this has always intrigued me. Rosemary Griffiths heard me mention the road on my BBC WM radio show and informed me that 'my father used to take me to school that way every day in the 1950s and 60s. He told me that it was named after a Victorian "lady novelist". I looked up the name on Google today and it came up with Princess Louise, sixth child and fourth daughter of Queen Victoria who married the Marquis of Lorne in 1871 in St. George's chapel, Windsor. He spent some years in Canada as Governor. She was reputed to be an accomplished writer, sculptor and artist (so perhaps that's where the novelist memory comes in).

'The marriage was childless and not particularly happy. He was reputed to be bisexual or homosexual. There is a rumour that Louise had one of the windows of Kensington Palace bricked up so that he could not "escape" and go cruising for soldiers in the park.'

Loveday Street, Gun Quarter

In July 1766 an advertisement appeared in *Aris's Birmingham Gazette* for 'Twelve New-built Houses, situate in Lovely Street, leading out of Steel-House Lane, now let at the Yearly Rent of £70, all well tenanted, and pleasantly situated, with a Yard entire, good soft-Water, and Gardening to each House, free from Ground Rent. For further Particulars enquire of Mr. Norman Mabbank, opposite Moat-Lane, in Digbeth who will shew the same.' These houses were in what would become known as Loveday Street. According to William Hutton, in the sixteenth century a John Cooper left four acres of land between Steelhouse Lane and Walmer Lane to make love days for the people of Birmingham. Joe McKenna writes that in the Middle Ages, Loveday was a Christian feast of reconciliation when the parish priest acted as a mediator in disputes. Rent from the croft was used to pay for the provide entertainment on this day – hence Loveday Croft. In 1907 the Birmingham Maternity Hospital was opened in Loveday Street. Thousands of Brummies were born there until it was closed in 1968.

An atmospheric photograph looking down Loveday Street in 1962. Steelhouse Lane and the end of the General Hospital are on the left. The island upon which the man is standing by the bollards was a major intersection and was known as Corporation Place. It brought together not only Loveday Street and Steelhouse Lane but also the upper and lower ends of Corporation Street, Lancaster Street, Aston Street, Vauxhall Street and Stafford Street. Today the James Watt Queensway has swept away that junction and the bottom of Steelhouse Lane and Corporation Street is now used mostly by visitors to the Children's Hospital (which now occupies the buildings of the old General Hospital).

Lovers Walk, Aston.

Lovers Walk, Aston

Lovers Walk still runs up from Lichfield Road from Aston Station, and alongside the railway line to Grosvenor Road. Its name suggests that once this was a country walk along which courting couples went. It is not shown on the Map of Aston Manor in 1833, but is obvious 50 years later on the Street Map of Aston Manor – although it is not named. A curious street, Lovers Walk had houses only down one side. **Medlicott Road**, Sparkbrook was **Love Lane** until 1888 when it was renamed after a landowner; whilst Love Lane, Duddeston recalled a Love Cottage on Dartmouth Street. In the later nineteenth century it was in one of the poorest neighbourhoods in Birmingham.

Lozells Road and Lozells Street, Lozells

Oozells Street off Broad Street and Lozells: they are two of the most intriguing names in Birmingham and fascinatingly they share the same second syllable. So what do they mean and are they connected? In the eighteenth century, the Oozells Estate was part of the wide lands of the Colmore family. Recalled in Colmore Row and Great Colmore Street, the Colmores owned much of central Birmingham, the Jewellery Quarter, the Holloway Head neighbourhood and the Summer Lane district. They lived in New Hall, hence Newhall Street, and the story goes that the Oozells holding was so named because Ann Colmore, who was an ardent gambler, lost it in a game of cards to a chap called Oozells – who was a French Huguenot (Protestant) who had fled France because of religious persecution.

However, in 1862 Arthur Ryland gave another explanation at a meeting of the Midland Counties Archaeological Association. His family owned much of Ladywood and he stated that from old deeds in his possession it appeared that the estate had belonged to the Odingsells family and that Oozells was a corruption of that name. This also seems unlikely as the Odingsells were lords of the manor of Solihull. Descended from a Flemish knight, they gained a market charter for their manor and also rebuilt the Church of Saint Alphege, but I have found no evidence that they owned land in Birmingham.

So the mystery of Oozells remains. And what of Lozells? A few years back when I was researching my book on the district names of Birmingham, David Tibbins thoughtfully wrote to me about a story he remembered from his childhood. He had lived in Lozells and used to run errands for two old ladies called Mrs Fletcher and Mrs Doody of 224, Lozells Road. They had told David that the area was called Lowcells – and that the latter part of the name was derived from two wells. One was in their garden and the second was in a garden in Church Street, on the right-hand side up from St Silas Square.

The ladies were certainly correct about the original spelling of Lozells. Recently David Cox wrote to me and told me that his Aston-born father moved to Lozells in the 1940s and 'was always interested in the history of the area, spending hours in libraries, churches etc doing research. Sadly he died in 1964. He used to keep all "old cuttings" from the newspaper regarding the history of the area.'

Numbers 175-195 Lozells Street in 1967. Look at those wonderful adverts on the huckster's shop on the corner.

David has kindly sent me two such cuttings. The first was a letter to the Mail from someone called F.W.P. He stated that he had in his possession an ancient map that featured a 'Lowe's Farm (hence Farm Street) from where Burbury Park now stands up to the present Wills Street and before the hill was dug away by Lewis and Company as a brick-making district there was a gentle slope of meadow land shown on the map as Lowe's Hills.' Other accounts declare that this name originated from Mr Lowe, the local farmer.

David's father replied to this letter explaining that the earliest known map of the Manor of Aston was that made by John Tomlinson in 1758. This indicated an area called "The Lowcells" which 'consisted mainly of a large farm, the buildings of which stood close to the main Lozells Road, then known as Lowcells Lane, on the land now remaining between Lozells Street and Carpenters Road. A large wood called "The Lowcells Wood" lay to the south where it was bounded by the Hockley Brook.' The earliest mention of the Losells Wood is in a deed from 1759. Importantly, older folk from the neighbourhood continue to pronounce Lozells without the 'e' whilst the 'z' is given as an 's'. Thus the sound is akin to that of Lowcells.

Mr Cox believed that Lozells was of Anglo-Saxon origin, from the words lowe (hill) and cele (cold), and hence meant the cold hills. The meaning of this name will be obvious to the local inhabitants. Joe McKenna, an expert on Birmingham place names, feels differently. He argues that Lozells may mean the hill of Lor, for a deed of 1546 refers to 'Lorres Hill, otherwise Lowsill'.

Lowsells Farm itself was sold in 1793, following the death of its owner Joseph Cooper. The property was declared to be valuable and improved, having a commodious farm house, large barn and stables, cow houses, stalls for feeding cattle, graineries, a blacksmith's shop and other out buildings. In addition there were well planted gardens and fourteen closes or pieces of rich arable, meadow or pasture land. The farm was still obvious on Fowler's Map of Aston Manor in 1833, but a few buildings were now present both on the Lozells Road in the forthcoming Carlyle Road district, and in the west where Brougham Street was indicated but not named.

Over the next twenty years, Lozells became a largely upper-working class neighbourhood and as elsewhere in urbanising Birmingham, the growing population was accompanied by the consecration of a new church. In this case it was Saint Silas, built in 1854. This was a year before the building of Saint Matthias, Wheeler Street which served the recently developed district of Hockley just across the brook which divided the two districts. Building work continued in Lozells, and between 1855-60 the Birmingham Freehold Land Society laid out the Wheeler Street Estate. Back-to-backs were not allowed and the locality was characterised by well-built homes with parlours and three bedrooms. Later in the nineteenth century, similar dwellings would fill Bournbrook, Sparkhill, Saltley, Small Heath, Bordesley Green, Gib Heath and other districts of Birmingham.

There were some back-to-backs in Lennox Street, Wheeler Street and elsewhere which were cleared in the 1960s, but the predominance of good quality homes

A view of Ludgate Hill in the 1930s from Church Street. The car is crossing Great Charles Street and in the background is Saint Paul's Church.

meant that Lozells has changed little in its layout and buildings since the 1860s. Mind you there is just one last interpretation to mention. According to Margaret Gelling, the renowned place name historian, in Middle English the word 'losel' meant someone who was a scoundrel or who was worthless. Who then was the scoundrel and why was he, or she, associated with the slopes leading up from the Hockley Brook? We'll never know. So like Oozells, the meaning of Lozells will always be swirled in a mist of mystery.

Ludgate Hill, Jewellery Quarter

It is a quiz question that is guaranteed to fox people: which football ground is the highest in the country. Invariably people plump for Blackburn or Halifax, close as they are to the Pennines, but the answer is actually the Hawthorns, the home of West Bromwich Albion. This may seem surprising, but West Bromwich lies on what geographers call the Birmingham Plateau. This is an upland area that has been cut off by the valleys of the Trent, Severn and Avon and their tributaries, and which has been split into the South Staffordshire and East Warwickshire plateaus by the valleys of the lower Tame and Blythe rivers.

The South Staffordshire Plateau itself can be divided into major units of based upon river basins, plateaus and ridges. Thus there are the: Cannock Chase High Plateau; the South Cannock Plateau; the Sutton Plateau; the Upper Tame Valley; the Sedgley-Northfield Ridge (including the Rowley Hills); the West Bromwich-

Harborne Plateau; the Clent-Lickey Ridge; the Stour Valley Plateau Fringe; the South Western Plateau Fringe; the Arrow Valley Plateau Fringe; and the Solihull plateau. The Sedgley-Northfield Ridge forms the main English watershed as far as Frankley Beeches. Springs and rivers on one side drain to the Bristol Channel and those on the east drain towards the North Sea. The highest point in this ridge is Turner's Hill at 866 feet. Most of Birmingham, however, actually stands on the West Bromwich-Harborne Plateau, which is similar in geology and relief to the eastern part of the Sutton Plateau. In both plateaus most of the surface lies between 400 and 500 feet above sea level, although Barr Beacon rises to over 700 feet.

Travelling up the M1 from Rugby, there is a terrific view of Birmingham lying ahead, looking as if it is on a flat plateau. It is in geographical terms, but that is not to say that there are not hills within Birmingham – for there are. Indeed, some people have jokingly declared that just as Rome, Birmingham is built upon seven hills. In fact the hills in the city centre area are all points rising above the red sandstone ridge that is above the Rea Valley for much of its length and which goes from Northfield to Sutton. It is matched by another ridge along which goes the Moseley Road from Camp Hill to the Maypole.

So what then are the hills of Birmingham? John Pegg contacted me and feels that six of them are Snow Hill, Constitution Hill, Summer Hill, Spring Hill, Ludgate Hill and Bennetts Hill but is 'never certain about the seventh'. This is an intriguing point of discussion. Because they are outside the original borough of Birmingham that developed after the market charter was granted in 1166 and thus the modern city centre, I would exclude the following hills: Camp Hill, Key Hill, Constitution Hill, and Spring Hill. I would therefore include Bennetts Hill, Easy Hill, Summer Hill, Holloway Head, Snow Hill and Newhall Hill and Ludgate Hill as one – thus giving six hills. To these I would add Singer's Hill.

This hill is only known today because of the name of the magnificent Singer's Hill Synagogue in Blucher Street. Indeed I have not come across any documentary evidence that mentions Singer's Hill. Some people might state that Singer's Hill is the same as Holloway Head; I would disagree. Singer's Hill is to the north of the road that is called Holloway Head and even now there is definite hill that rises up from Suffolk Street, as is indicated by the steepness of Gough Street. The hill that I would call Holloway Head lies to the south west of the road of the same title and heads up from Bristol Street and the valley of the River Rea as made plain by Lee Bank Middleway.

Bradford's map of 1750 shows Easy Hill and indicates a road called Snow Hill (formerly Sandy Lane); and Hanson's Map of 1781 adds two more roads on hills. They are Holloway Head and **Newhall Hill** – although at various times this was also known as **Camden Hill** and **Harper's Hill**. Newhall was so named after the home of the Colmores (see Colmore Row). Hanson also names **Ludgate Street** going down from Great Charles Street and parallel with Newhall Street. In effect then Ludgate Hill is the same as Newhall Hill. Hutton, in his *History of Birmingham*, deduced that Ludgate Hill was an imitation of the place in London.

In 1810, Kempson brought out a map for the Street Commissioners of Birmingham and this indicated both Constitution Hill and Summer Hill. This latter was a road but was just called Summer Hill. The map also shows a space of land called Key Hill between Great Hampton Street and Icknield Street, and another named New Hall Hill. This rose to the west of Newhall Street and by George Street. The road called **Newhall Hill** would soon be cut out through the hill, going up from the Parade and the Sandpits to Frederick Street. As for Bennetts Hill it emerged just after the Napoleonic Wars ended in 1815. So seven hills there are – just like Rome. (See also Bennetts Hill, Holloway Head, Key Hill, Snow Hill, and Summer Hill).

Lyndon Road, Sheldon

Lyndon Road runs into the Coventry Road opposite Horse Shoes Lane, Wells Green and is mostly in Solihull. Its name is an interesting one. There is a also a Lyndon in Leicestershire and its meaning is given as the hill ('dun') where either lime trees or flax ('lin' or 'lind') is grown. Lyndon, Warwickshire was first recorded as Linde in 1221, as Lyndene in 1262 and Lyndone by 1317. The 1262 spelling complicates matters for whilst 'Lynd' still means either flax or lime tree, then 'dene' signifies a valley. This latter interpretation is preferred by Joe McKenna and it seems to have weight given that Lyndon is on the slopes leading down to the River Cole.

In the early twentieth century, the main buildings locally were Lyndon Farm, close to the later Larne Road; the nearby Saint Bernard's Grange on Barrow's Lane; the Manor House on Manor House Lane; and Gilbertstone (see Gilbertstone Road). A detached part of Bickenhill, Lyndon and Lyndon Green became part of Sheldon and thus were incorporated into Birmingham in 1931. The district was developed rapidly with private housing and had become built up by 1939.

M

Macdonald Street, Highgate

It's a long way from the stunning green glens of Antrim to the blackened back streets of Brummagem – but that great distance in miles and feeling is bridged by a clutch of streets in and around Highgate. Macdonald Street is the chief of them, for it recalls a William Macdonald, whose father, Roger, hailed from Belfast, and whose ancestors were Antrim people. The family was well established in the north east of Ireland, and claimed descent from the members of the Highland clan MacDonald that had settled in Antrim from at least the sixteenth century.

Roger and his wife, Mary, came to Birmingham in the 1780s. They were most unusual, as there is little evidence of other Irish people in our town in the eighteenth century. The presence of a James Wright from Dublin in 1723 is indicated by Birmingham's certificates of settlement for the forty years from 1686; and in his Autobiography, Alexander Carlyle mentions that when he visited Birmingham in about 1760 he met with a Patrick Downy, an apprentice to the wealthy manufacturer, Samuel Garbett. Although Downy's name suggests that he may have been Irish there is no hard evidence to verify this.

So what made Roger and Mary Macdonald move to Birmingham? We do not know, but whatever the case they did well. Of their five sons and two daughters, there is information on three of the lads: Joseph was born in 1787 and became a nail manufacturer, whilst John, who was 23 years younger, went on to run a leather supply and cutting business. However it was William, who was born in 1797 and baptised at St Martin's in the Bull Ring, who became known as 'the wealthy Macdonald'.

Mind you at one stage it did not look like that William would have any future in Birmingham. The family story goes that he made lots of money from land and property deals in Birmingham before going out to New South Wales to make more money in property. The reality was very different. A gunsmith and silver plater, William fell foul of the law and was transported to Australia as a convicted felon.

In March 1820, when he was just 22, he was charged with nine others of uttering forged Bank of England notes. This was a capital offence and was treated harshly by the State. Just eight years before, on 28 March 1812 the military had attacked the fortified farm of William Booth in Perry Barr. After his capture, the soldiers found £3,000 in good notes, 200 guineas in gold, £600 in counterfeit silver coins and a large amount of forged notes. Booth was sent for trial at Stratford Assizes. Found guilty he was executed publicly on 15 August 1815, but the hangman bungled the job and so the false coiner had to be revived and hanged again two hours later. He was buried at Handsworth Old Church and later moved.

With regard to Macdonald's case, eight of his co-defendants pleaded guilty to the lesser charge of having forged notes in their possession and were sentenced to transportation to Australia for fourteen years. Macdonald and Charles Clarke eschewed this route and were found guilty of forgery. Clarke was sentenced to death, but as upon reflection he had wanted to plead guilty, the judge extended mercy. As for William Macdonald, however, he 'had obstinately resisted every attempt to persuade him to adopt a similar step' and so the law took its harsh and unforgiving course.

Fortunately, Macdonald was not hung – although he was sentenced to transportation for life, in itself regarded as a death sentence by all those who never would see their loved ones or homeland again. In Australia he joined another of his brothers, Edward, who had also been in the gun trade and who had been convicted the previous year of disposing of forged banknotes and had been sentenced to fourteen years transportation.

At first William Macdonald was sent to the Airds district and was assigned as a servant. That did not last long. A short man, not much more than five feet in height, he must have been gutsy and full of resolve and by 1824 he had set himself up in business in Sydney as an ironmonger and gunmaker. The next year he began the Colony's first shot manufactory and he successfully petitioned the Governor of the Colony for his wife, Elizabeth, and their son, William Edward, to join him. Baptised at Saint John's in Deritend in 1819, this son is recalled in William Edward Street.

A view along Macdonald Street from the 'White Horse', a Dare's Brewery house, on the corner of Bishop Street, 1930s.

Elizabeth, too, must have been strong of character to have sailed across the world in dangerous seas with a young child and to an uncertain future. United, the couple went on to have four children in Australia between 1827 and 1832. They were Angelina, Emily, Charles Henry and Adelaide. They are brought to mind in Angelina Street, Emily Street, Charles Henry Street and Adelaide Street.

William's brother, Edward, also went into the gun trade in Australia but he kept on getting himself into trouble with the authorities, and after making an escape attempt from his exile, he was jailed for a long stretch. By contrast, William did well. He opened up 'The Birmingham and Sheffield Cutlery and Ironmongery Warehouse' in George Street, where he sold guns and everything that was needed by a gunmaker; he operated his own brass foundry; and he invested in land and moved into property dealing.

Then in 1828 William received a conditional pardon, after he was supported in his petition by reputable citizens who stated that 'he is possessed of considerable property which he has realised by his industry and his conduct appears to have been remarkably good.' Three years later he was granted an absolute pardon, which allowed him the right to return to England. He did so in 1838 as 'a gentleman', someone who did not need to work and who had gained a high social standing. It was a remarkable transformation from his low point as a felon who had escaped the death sentence.

Macdonald settled first at Bristol House in Bristol Street, Birmingham and then from 1846 at the Poplars on the Stratford Road in Sparkbrook, hence Poplar Road. Quickly he began to buy land in Highgate, where there still is a Macdonald Street, and Hockley, where there was another Macdonald Street that was re-named **Frankfort Street** in 1881. He died in 1852 aged 54, a wealthy man. His immediate estate was valued at £33,610 – at a time when a skilled working man would be lucky to earn £100 a year and when a labourer would be hard pressed to pull in half that amount. But it seems that this fabulous amount did not include the value of freeholds and other assets held both in Birmingham and Sydney, where there was a Macdonald Buildings. This was a large commercial structure in Sydney.

His wife, Elizabeth, died four years later. Both are interred in the Macdonald family vault in Key Hill Cemetery, Hockley. Their sons William Edwards and Charles Henry died before their mid 30s.

I dedicate this section to the memory of the late Ray Slater, whose indefatigable research into the Macdonald family he shared generously with me. Ray's great grandmother was born Mary Anne Macdonald in 1840. She was the granddaughter of Joseph, a brother of William Macdonald 'the wealthy'. Ray's sister, Diana, also worked hard at uncovering the family connection by obtaining a lot of material from Australia and I also pay tribute to her.

Machin Road, Erdington

Between the Sutton New Road and Summer Road, Machin Road takes its name from a man who was a councillor and churchwarden locally.

Magdala Street, Winson Green

A little cul-de-sac off the Winson Green Road and just before Birmingham Prison, Magdala recalls a battle in Abyssinia (Ethiopia) 1868. Emperor Téwodros II was a moderniser who built roads, introduced mail, and manufactured his country's first cannon. He welcomed skilled workers and travellers from Germany, France and England and in 1864 he offered an alliance to Britain. When he had no reply after two years the Emperor jailed the British consul and other Britons. A British envoy was sent and he and his party were also imprisoned. Consequently a military force was sent to Abyssinia under Robert Napier, breech-loaded rifles against Ethiopian muskets. It defeated the Ethiopians. Emperor Téwodros committed suicide and the British commander was made Lord Robert Napier of Magdala.

Market Street, City

This is a most unusual street. Going between Bromsgrove Street and Upper Dean Street, it ran between Jamaica Row and Dean Street and was an unadopted road – that is the Council had no obligation to carry out any work to repair or maintain the surface, responsibility for any repairs or maintenance work lying with the owners/occupiers.

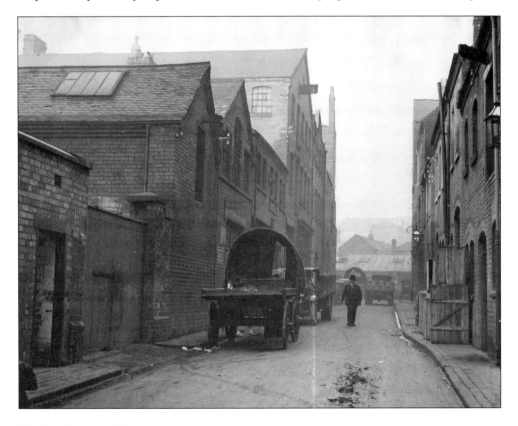

Market Street in 1933.

According to Kelly's Directory, in 1856 it was the location of Earles Optical Co., manufacturing opticians; Wholesale Hardwares Ltd; Hawkesford & Son, Wholesale tobacconist; J. V. White & Co. Ltd.; fruit salesmen; and Randall Bros. & Parsons Ltd fruit merchants. It also had the goods' entrances for Henry Wood & Sons toy dealers and Johnsons (Warehousemen) Ltd. Probably named after the nearby Smithfield Market, it disappeared in the late 1960s/early 1970s when the present Wholesale Markets complex was built.

Market Street, Duddeston

A short street coming off Coleshill Street, Market Street went into Hicks Square, itself lying between Prince's Street and Nova Scotia Street. Running parallel with Market Street were Doe Street to the west and the rest of Prince's Street to the west. They were amongst a clutch of streets in this neighbourhood that were noticeable for their shortness. It took its name from the New Market Hall, which was erected in 1837 by Messrs E. and C. Robins in Prospect Row. They may have been related to the Josiah Robins who is shown as extensive landowner on Lord Dartmouth's Map of 1824 and 1825. This also indicates that Hicks Square was on the edge of the countryside, something that had changed by the time that the new market hall was built.

Market Street and Hicks Square in 1963.

The two Robins were keen to tap into the increasing population on this side of Birmingham and the story goes that they first attempted to cover the old open air market at Gosta Green. Bits were put up and as quickly were taken down by the local folk who resented the moves, forcing the Robins to move to a market that they had built a little further down from Gosta Green. They divided their building into 'compartments for the sale of provisions', but it did not take off and later became a warehouse and was noticeable as a triangle of land between Prospect Row, AB Row, Cardigan Street, Howe Street and Belmont Row. Like most of the other little streets hereabouts, Market Street fell before the development both of Aston University and Jennens Row as a dual carriageway. There is also the small **New Market Street** that comes off Cornwall Street and goes into Great Charles Queensway. It is said that there was an open air market here in the 1780s, when the site was on the edge of Birmingham, and indeed Hanson's Map of 1791 does include a Newhall Market.

Martineau Street, City

There is a cracking Birmingham monologue that Mark Evetts of the Birmingham Icknield Male Voice Choir often recites to the delight of Brummie audiences. It tells the story of Old Bill, a big, bluff and blustery copper who patrolled the town back

The redevelopment of Martineau Street in 1960.

in the late 1800s. Not the brightest of sparks, Bill was a diligent if unimaginative policeman. One day as pounded his beat he came upon a right palaver in a certain street. There were crowds milling about and carts and wagons of every description were backing up and down the road.

Slowly but surely Bill made his way through the commotion, his movements as rounded as was his girth. At last he reached the cause of all the bother. There splayed out upon the ground was a horse that had drawn its last breath. It was still attached to a cart and the carter himself was standing disconsolate at the loss of his animal and mithered at the hustle and bustle around him. Old Bill took no cotter of the calls to 'sort it out!' and 'let's get cracking, there's work to be done!' Ponderously he took out his pencil and notepad and began to take down all the particulars of the affair.

At what seemed like a snail's place he finally came to his last question. He had not noticed what street he was in and looking about him he could find no sign to alert him. So he looked at the carter and asked him where they stood. The workman readily replied 'Martineau Street', unaware that was the worst thing he could have uttered. Upon hearing the name Old Bill suddenly quickened his movements. He thrust his pencil and notepad back into his uniform and ordered the carter to pick up the horse and drag it to the next street. Why, because Old Bill could not spell Martineau Street!

Pronounced by Brummies as Martinoo, Martineau Street commemorates a remarkable family that has made a major impact upon our city. Descended from Huguenots, Protestants, who fled religious persecution in France in the late 1600s, they had settled in Norwich. Then in 1828 one of them came to Birmingham. He was Robert Martineau, the nephew of Harriet Martineau, the famous writer and journalist. Robert was drawn to the Midlands by his marriage to Jane Smith, the daughter of Samuel Smith, co-partner in the Eagle Foundry on Broad Street.

George Jacob Holyoake was a famous Birmingham campaigner for working-class rights and he worked at the Eagle in the 1830s. He recalled Smith as 'a Unitarian, a placid gentleman. The men were always glad when it fell to him to pay them, as he had a kindly word for them, and would sometimes make them small advances when the wages of the piece-workers fell low.' By contrast his partner, William Hawkes, was harsh, exacting and flint-hearted.

Arriving in Birmingham, Robert Martineau went into business as a manufacturer and he became a notable figure who settled with his wife on the Bristol Road in Edgbaston and was elected mayor in 1846. Their son, Thomas (later Sir Thomas), was born in 1828 and was educated at the Birmingham and Edgbaston Proprietary School. In 1844 he was articled to Arthur Ryland, a well-known local solicitor of Birmingham with whom he became a partner in 1851. The successor business is Martineau Johnson, which is based in the city centre and which is one of the United Kingdom's leading independent law firms.

Holder of the prestigious office of law clerk of the Birmingham Assay Office, Thomas Martineau was a successful lawyer. He became as successful in the civic life of Birmingham. An active Liberal, he became a close friend of Joseph Chamberlain through their membership of the Birmingham and Edgbaston Debating Society and in 1860 he married Emily Kenrick, daughter Timothy Kenrick of the important hardware firm in West Bromwich.

Both families were Unitarians, members of a small but influential and economically powerful Non-Conformist sect that did not believe in the Trinity of God the Father, God the Son and God the Holy Ghost. Significantly, Emily's sisters married Joseph Chamberlain and Charles Gabriel Beale, each of whom was to be of profound importance to Birmingham. These close relationships deepened the bond between the leading Unitarians in the town.

In 1876, Thomas Martineau was voted on to the Council. Six years later he was elected an alderman, and in 1884 he became mayor – a post to which he was re-elected in the next two years. Martineau's legal expertise was invaluable to the work of the Council and he helped to steer through Parliament the scheme for building reservoirs in the Elan Valley, so as to supply Birmingham with fresh water. His other great achievement was as a proponent of making Birmingham an assize town, whereby it had a county court. This was achieved in 1884 and three years later Queen Victoria laid the foundation stone of the magnificent Victoria Law Courts in Corporation Street. This was her jubilee year and she was received by Martineau as mayor. Within two days of the ceremony he was knighted at Windsor. Soon after Sir Thomas's health began to decline and he died in 1893 at his home in Edgbaston.

He was followed in his public service by his son, Ernest, who was also a solicitor with Ryland and Martineau and who was Lord Mayor in 1912 and 1913. He resigned his office in September 1914 when he joined up in the First World War, becoming Lieutenant Colonel of 6th Battalion Royal Warwickshire (Territorial) Regiment. Returning to public life in peace-time, Ernest Martineau was accorded the greatest honour that can be given by Birmingham when he was made a freeman of the borough in 1938.

Two years later, his son, Wilfred Martineau, became Lord Mayor. Later knighted, he is brought to mind by Sir Wilfred Martineau School – thus named because of his work as chairman of the Education Committee on the Council. Noted as a staunch supporter of investment in schools and as a director of the Birmingham Repertory Theatre, Sir Wilfred was followed on the council in turn by his son, Denis Martineau. Lord Mayor in 1986-7, Denis was one of the last of the old Birmingham middle-class families to serve his city. He did so with distinction and dedication. I was honoured to have met him and to have gained from his knowledge.

Named after Sir Thomas in particular, Martineau Street recalled this remarkable family. It emerged in 1886 and traffic passed along it for the last time on 15 October 1960. The street then disappeared to be replaced by Martineau Square, and in turn that has gone to make way for the development of the new Martineau Galleries. Let us not forget that it is named after a family whose guiding light was that of serving the people of Birmingham.

Mason Road, Erdington

Josiah Mason knew what it was to have to collar and get on through his own endeavours. The second son of a Kidderminster carpet weaver called Josiah Mason and his wife Elizabeth Griffiths, when he was just eight Josiah traipsed the streets of the Worcestershire town selling bread and cakes. He went on to hawk fruit and vegetables that he carried on a donkey. Mind you he was not to remain as a street seller for long, for Josiah was resolved to improve himself intellectually and financially. Somehow he taught himself to write and with the money he made from his little business he bought himself books on science, theology and history. Next he enrolled at the local Unitarian Sunday School.

As much as he was grasping at knowledge he was also seeking to get on and tried his hand as a shoemaker, blacksmith, carpenter, painter and carpet weaver. None of them allowed him to become financially independent and so in 1816 he went to Birmingham to visit his uncle, Richard Griffiths. The manager of the Aston Flint Glass Works, Griffiths had also invested in a jewellery and toymaking business and after a dispute with his partner he put Josiah in charge of things. Marrying Richard's daughter, Anne, Mason' was on the up. A prickly character, he fell out with his uncle in 1822 and became manager for Samuel Harrison, a split ring manufacturer in Lancaster Street. Harrison was a typical Brummie, innovative, inventive and ingenious. He invented the split ring for holding keys and is thought by some to have been the first to make steel pen nibs in Birmingham.

Mason and Harrison became great friends and in 1823 when the older man retired, Josiah Mason bought the firm for £500, which was to be in installments of £100. A hard and seemingly tireless worker Mason improved efficiency at the works and introduced stamping machines to make the split rings. Previously these had been made by hand. Things went well and after five years Josiah extended the factory. By then he had begun making pens in a small way and in 1829 he was the first person to make cedar pen holders. That year he spotted some pens in a shop in Bull Street that had been made by James Perry, a stationer of London. Mason was certain that he could do better, so he bought one and took it home. A skilled worker himself, Mason produced three pens that night which he sent to Perry. Impressed, Perry came to Birmingham to meet Mason and immediately and signed a contract which meant that Mason would make all of Perry's pens.

The first order of 100 gross of pens was made by about twelve workpeople and necessitated the rolling of one hundredweight of steel in a week. They were sent to London on 20 November 1830. Mason's business in Lancaster Street waxed, although he made few pens under his own name, and when he retired at the age of 80 in 1875 he was employing over 1,000 people. By then his factory was largest in the world for making pen-nibs and it required the rolling of three tons week exceeded 3 tons. About one and a half million pens were produced from each ton of steel.

Mason was multi-faceted and was involved in other business ventures. In 1844 George Elkington patented the use of cyanides of gold and silver in electroplating. It was a revolutionary process that would speed and make more efficient the previously laborious task of plating gold and silver on to base metal; however Elkington needed money to develop the business. He and his cousin Henry Elkington gained that investment from Mason and were able to electroplate spoons, forks, and other articles with Elkington. Copper wire was essential for electroplating and to secure their supply of the metal the Elkington and Mason built a copper smelting works at Pembrey in Carmarthenshire, Wales. Nickel was the metal upon which gold or silver was electroplated and accordingly Mason joined with the inventor Alexander Parkes to establish the world's first nickel manufacturing works in Erdington.

Perhaps because of the illnesses he suffered in the 1840s, Mason sold his pen company to George Elkington, but bought it back in 1852. Thirteen years later Mason pulled out of active involvement in the electroplating business. By this stage, he had gained a reputation for philanthropy. In 1858 he opened almshouses in Station Road, Erdington for spinsters and widows over 50 and for orphan girls. These premises came to be inadequate and in 1869 a second, larger orphanage was opened in **Bell Lane**, now called **Orphanage Road**. It had rooms for 26 women and dormitories for 300 children. He found all the money for the huge Italianate building that was dominated by three tall towers and cost £60,000 to build and was endowed to the tune of £200,000. A new wing was added later so that a total 500 children, including 150 boys, might be to be accommodated.

Mason's giving came with demands. Deeply infused with strict moral codes, he decreed that there should be no restrictions based upon locality, nationality or religious belief but that only legitimate children whose parents were dead could be admitted to the orphanage. Conditions were harsh. The youngsters slept in large dormitories and were allowed only two visits a year, each of two hours; the diet was unvaried; and the children were worked hard at chores. Later redesignated a school, the orphanage became too big to maintain and it was closed by its trustees in 1963. The site is now occupied by an estate of houses and the Yenton School. With the proceeds from the sale the trustees built a peaceful complex for elderly in Olton called **Mason Court**. He is also brought to mind in Mason Road, Erdington – a short road between Edwards Road and the High Street.

Perhaps Mason's most important and enduring contribution to the life of Birmingham came about in 1870 when he drew up trust deeds for a college of science. He intended that its students would go on to serve West Midland's industry and so the curriculum was confined to maths, physics, chemistry, natural sciences, physiology and engineering. Literature and theology were specifically excluded. The college, was built in Edmund Street and Great Charles Street at a cost of £170,000, including endowments, and was opened in 1880. Two of its early graduates were Stanley Baldwin and Neville Chamberlain, both of whom became prime ministers.

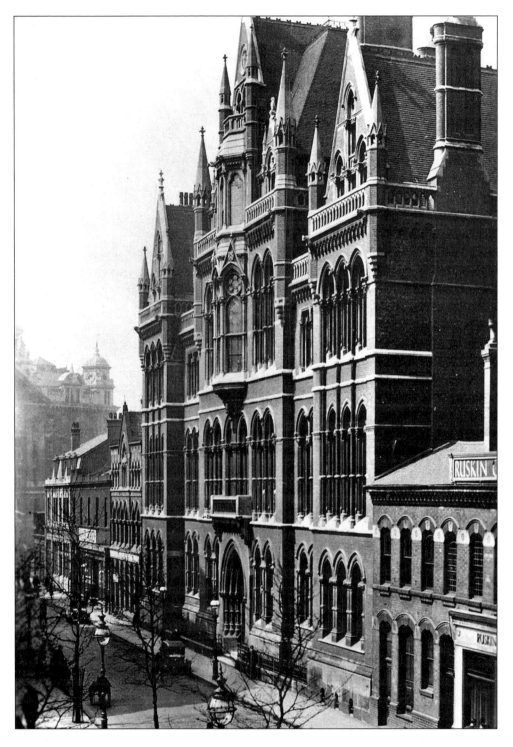

The magnificent Mason College in Edmund Street, destroyed to make way for the Central Library and Paradise Forum. It was a bad exchange.

In 1882 Mason's College absorbed the medical faculty of Queen's College (see Cox Street West). Six years later it became Mason's University College and then in 1900, the University of Birmingham. Mason's heraldic crest of a mermaid, forms part of the coat of arms of the university. Because of the development of a campus university at Edgbaston and the redevelopment of Birmingham city centre, in 1964 the Mason's College buildings were knocked down to make way for the new central library.

Knighted in 1872, two years after the death of his wife, Mason died nine years later at Norwood House, Erdington. His estate was valued at £51,729 5s. 7d. During his life he had given away the massive sum of nearly £500,000 and was commemorated by a statue in Edmund Street. This was removed in 1952 and instead a bronze bust of Mason now sits above a stone pillar in the middle of the roundabout at the junction of Chester Road and Orphanage Road, Erdington. Regarded rightly as an enigma by his biographer Brian Jones, Mason was disliked as a miser by his workpeople and would argue over pennies in a shop; yet he was also one of the most generous of Birmingham's benefactors – although he let folk know it.

Maryvale Road, Bournville

Heading up from Stirchley to Rowheath, this is supposed to take its name from a young woman called Mary Vale, who was a nurse to the children of the Stock family. However, David Jones feels that there may be a connection with his family, for one of his ancestors was a George Vale who married a Mary Middleton in 1820 at Kings Norton Parish Church. The 1861 Census gives George as a scuttle maker, but the Trades Directory indicates that he was also a farmer. He and his wife, Mary Vale, lived at Bredon Cross – not far away from Bournville and David wonders whether this Mary gave her name to Maryvale Road.

The Stocks were farmers who had owned four of the five farms taken over by the Cadburys when they moved their chocolate works to 'the factory in a garden' in Kings Norton in 1878/9. These were Two Gates Farm by the junction of Sycamore Road and Willow Road; Bournbrook Farm by the cross-roads of Linden Road and Bournville Lane; Row Heath Farm, at the meeting of Franklin Road and Oak Tree Lane, hence **Rowheath Road**; Bournbrook Hall Farm, which later became the Girls' Recreation Ground at Cadbury's; and Lea House Farm, Stirchley (see Lea House Road). The Stocks live on in **Stocks Wood**, off Acacia Road in Bournville.

Masshouse Circus, City

Birmingham grew slowly but surely from the time in gained a market charter in 1166, but in the last quarter its growth accelerated. Little research has been done on this vital period but it provided the base for the spectacular rise of the town in the 1700s. William Hutton, Birmingham's first historian, was certain of the reason for its remarkable increase in population, size and fame:

In a town like Birmingham, unfettered with charteral laws; which gives access to the stranger of every denomination, for he here finds a freedom by birthright; and where the principles of toleration are well understood, it is no wonder we find various modes of worship. The wonder consists in finding such *agreement*, in such variety. We have fourteen places for religious exercise, six of the established church, three dissenting meeting houses, a Quakers, Baptist, Methodist, Roman Catholic, and Jewish. Two of these only are churches, of which elsewhere.

Hutton regarded Birmingham as a free town. It had no charter of incorporation (until 1838), no bishop and no gilds as did places Coventry and Nottingham, the expansion of which were stifled by self-serving organisations. His interpretation has been taken up by many historians, who focus upon the movement into Birmingham of people who dissented from the beliefs of the Church of England. These Dissenters became known as Non-Conformists and included Quakers like the Lloyds and Cadburys and Unitarians such as the Kenricks and Chamberlains. Denied access to the law, the army, the Royal Navy and the church by religious discrimination as much as by their own principles, many Dissenters moved into manufacturing and commerce and their positive impact on the development of Birmingham should not be dismissed or diminished.

For all that it is important not to neglect the significance of Anglican manufacturers such as Matthew Boulton, whilst is should also be noted that the majority of Birmingham's working class were Church of England. Of course there were many Baptists and Methodists and they were influential, but Methodism was never as powerful a force in the City as it was in the Black Country. Most English Brummies hailed from families, like my own, that had moved here from the villages of north Warwickshire and north Worcestershire, where Anglican affiliation was pronounced. In the later nineteenth and early twentieth centuries, this mostly Church of England working class was ruled by a numerically small but politically and economically strong Non-Conformist elite drawn from the ranks of Quakers and Unitarians.

By this period religious tolerance in Birmingham was a noticeable phenomenon, and indeed some historians trace this tolerance back to the early seventeenth century; and in the English Civil War (see Rupert Street), most of Birmingham's people came out for the cause of Parliament. However, there wee occasions when the Anglican poor were stirred up by Anglican gentry into violence against religious minorities. The most noteworthy were the Priestley Riots of 1791, but another smirch in our history was in the anti-Catholic riots of 1689.

Following the Reformation and the so-called Glorious Revolution of 1688, Catholics were discriminated against and often persecuted as recusants (see Oscott Road and Middlemore Road). Called recusants because they refused to conform to the Church of England, which was established by law as the church of the land, Catholics locally diminished in numbers. The first recusant roll of 1592-3 noted that Handsworth, Northfield and Yardley each had four recusants. There is no information on the Warwickshire parishes that came to be part of Birmingham.

In 1676 a Census was taken under the auspices of Bishop Compton, Bishop of London. It recorded 101 Catholics (derogatorily termed papists) out of a population of 502 in Handsworth, which included Oscott. Elsewhere numbers were very low: there were eleven out of 2,623 folk in Birmingham; thirteen out of 1,531 in Aston; nineteen out of 1,082 in Kings Norton; six out of 309 in Northfield; and four out of 168 at Yardley. No Catholics were recorded in Sheldon and there are no figures for Harborne or Edgbaston. The figures given may have been too high for Handsworth at 20% and too low for the other parishes. Be that as it may, by the time of the Census a Franciscan had been ministering in the Birmingham neighbourhood for the previous twenty years, and another priest was tried in 1679 for celebrating mass in and around Oscott.

The Franciscan was Leo Randolph. He came to Birmingham in 1657 and 30 years later made the town the official seat of his mission. The same year, 1687, a cruciform chapel was built in what would be named Masshouse Lane. It was dedicated to St. Mary Magdalene, and had side chapels to St. Francis and the Virgin. Construction was enabled by 342 donations. These included timber from the Catholic king James II, money from Catholic gentry, and small gifts from Protestants. In March 1688 a convent was also begun. Both it and the church were burnt down in November the next year.

Randolph said that a rabble was instigated by Lord Delamere and that this mob were the culprits, although 'the better sort' looked on. According to tradition Randolph continued to minister to his flock, saying mass in Smallbrook Street. However after a short time he but he removed to Edgbaston where he established another chapel, whence he moved to a farmhouse further from the centre of the village. From 1688 the succession of priests was almost continuous and the Franciscan Mission moved back to Birmingham in the late eighteenth century (see St Chad's Queensway).

Masshouse Lane used to run from Dale End to the meeting of Park Street, Albert Street and Duddeston Row. The redevelopments of the 1960s threw it into the miskin of history but a great traffic island emerged above its site and was called Masshouse Circus. This itself was taken down in the early twenty-first century and now there is nothing to recall Masshouse Lane. However, nearby there is a strange, short and narrow passage that does bring it to mind. This is **Pater Noster Row**. Now merely a stub of a street coming off Park Street it may recall the fact that the Catholic mass was in Latin – for 'Pater Noster' is the Latin for 'Our Father'; the first words of the Lord's Prayer.

Maypole Lane, Highters Heath

Going from High Street, Solihull Lodge to Bell's Lane, Druids Heath, Maypole Lane is supposed to have been named after a man's generosity. The story is told that stranger got lost on the Drew's Heath (see Druids Lane) and was helped on his way by a local. In thanks the stranger put up on the heath a tall painted signpost with four arms indicating the directions to Birmingham, Kings Norton, Solihull and Alcester. This post was also used as a maypole and in the 1850s was replaced by proper maypole.

Metropolitan Road, Saltley

Joseph Wright was a canny and forward-thinking businessman. A leading stage-coach builder and the operator of most of the coaches between London and Birmingham, he quickly realised the coming of railways signalled the end of horse-drawn carriages. He was not downhearted, for swiftly he grasped the opportunity for making carriages for locomotives. In 1844 he patented improvements to four, six and eight-wheeled bogies and soon after he took the big decision to shift his base to Brum. The line to London and the North West had opened fully in 1838 and it was obvious that Birmingham was going to become the centre of England's rail network.

Within three years Wright had taken over another 50 acres and by 1853 he was giving work to 800 talented men. These skilled lads built rolling stock not only for England but also for Egypt, Sweden, India, Australia and a host of other countries. They were not on their own – the Saltley district was renowned makers of railway carriages. Down at Adderley Park was Brown and Marshall's. A Brummagem firm, they had also been stage coach makers, based in New Canal Street, and had moved to Saltley in 1853. From their new Britannia Works they designed and crafted the Peninsular and Oriental Express dining cars in 1892.

Ten years later, the company was amalgamated with Joseph Wright's business, now known as the Metropolitan, as well as a number of others across the country. Together they formed the Metropolitan Amalgamated Railway Carriage and Wagon Company Limited. In 1908, Brown and Marshall's business was transferred to the Saltley Works and its Britannia Works was then sold to the Wolseley Motor Car Company and later the Morris Commercial.

Up the road in Washwood Heath another railway carriage maker remained independent. This was the Midland Railway Carriage and Wagon Company Limited. Formed in Birmingham about 1844, initially it supplied to coal owners and others railway wagons that it had bought. Then in 1864 then Midland began manufacturing itself. Quickly, the business pioneered wagon leasing and the hire purchase of wagons. Thirty years later, it bought 62 acres of land from Lord Norton off Leigh Road, Washwood Heath.

In 1919, the Midland was bought by Cammell Laird and ten years later joined the great combine of the Metropolitan-Cammell Carriage and Wagon Works, which included Joseph Wright's old firm. During the Second World War, the Met as a whole became the biggest supplier of fighting tanks in the country, building a greater variety of tanks than elsewhere. Many of these ingenious tanks were used successfully in the D Day landings in Normandy and in crossing the Rhine. The Met was also a major supplier of radar mechanical equipment, producing many such vehicles at Saltley.

The workers of the Met stood foursquare in the battle for our freedom but sadly that counted for nothing in 2004 when the last of the workers there were laid off. Despite a strong order book and success at making the Pendolino tilting carriages for

Virgin Trains and despite a massive public protest, the French owners of the Met, Alstom, closed down these historic works. Sadly, not even Metropolitan Road now exists to remind us of the coach builders of Birmingham.

Middlemore Road, Northfield

The Middlemores were loyal to their faith and they paid a heavy price for their loyalty in money and life, but however grievously they suffered they held fast to their pride and integrity. Associated with Birmingham, Hawkesley, Hazelwell and Edgbaston, all the Middlemores claim descent from a John de Middlemore who is noted in documents relating to Studley and Solihull in the early thirteenth century and who may have been connected to the legal profession. His grandson was Thomas Middlemore. A citizen and merchant of London, he was married to Isabel Edgbastons, heiress to the manor of Edgbaston. In 1392 the inquiry into the founding of the Gild of the Holy Cross in Birmingham (see King Edwards Road) mentioned that it would be endowed with lands in Edgbaston that were held by Thomas de Middlemore from the heirs of John de Birmingham.

After Middlemore's death, his widow married John de Clodeshale, Lord of Saltley (see Clodeshall Road). Their third and only surviving daughter married Robert Arden of Park Hall, Castle Bromwich, who belonged to the ancient Warwickshire family to which Shakespeare's mother was to be connected (see Arden Road). By Thomas Middlemore, Isabel had eight children. They included, John, who inherited the manor of Edgbaston and Nicholas, who founded the Middlemores of Hawkesley. Their younger sister, Joan, became a nun and rose to be a prioress of a convent near to

Middlemore Road, Northfield in the early twentieth century.

Knowle. They gained the manor through the marriage of Nicholas Middlemore to the heiress of the Hawkeslow family (see Hawkesley Square).

John Middlemore passed Edgbaston to his son, Richard. He died in 1503 and was buried in the churchyard of St. Bartholomew, Edgbaston. In his will he left a small sum 'for the repair of that church, and the like sums to the Cathedral Church of St. Cedde, of Lichfield, the gild of the Holy Cross of Byrmyncham, the gild of St. John of Deryten', whilst six pounds of wax were to be burnt on the day of his funeral. Richard was married to Margery, daughter of Sir Thomas Throckmorton, of Coughton, near Studley. After she became a widow she took a solemn vow of chastity.

Her son, Thomas, and then her grandson, Robert, thereafter held Edgbaston. Robert lived through turbulent and dangerous times. Henry VIII broke with the Catholic Church over the refusal of the Pope to give him a divorce from Catherine of Aragon and so allow him to marry Anne Boleyn. Enraged, Henry secretly married Anne in 1533 and later that year was excommunicated by the Pope. The next year the Succession Act required peers, MPs and clergy to swear an oath that they accepted the right of succession to the throne of children arising from Henry's union with Anne; and the Act of Supremacy confirmed Henry as supreme head of the Church in England.

Humphrey Middlemore probably belonged to the Edgbaston family and may have been a son of Richard Middlemore and Margery Throckmorton. He was a martyr to his faith. A Carthusian monk at the Charterhouse, London he refused to take the oath as made law by the Act of Succession – a stand shared by his vicar, Father John Houghton. Both men were imprisoned in the Tower of London. After a month they were persuaded to take the oath conditionally and were released. The next year Father John was executed for refusing to take the new oath of supremacy, and Father Humphrey became vicar of the Charterhouse. Thomas Bedyll, one of the royal commissioners, came back to the monastery and strove to shake the faith of Father Humphrey and his community in the papal supremacy. He failed and so obtained authority to arrest the vicar and two other monks. He is recalled in Humphrey Middlemore Drive on the borders of Harborne and Edgbaston and by the Queen Elizabeth Hospital.

In prison the men were bound to posts with chains round their necks and legs for two weeks. Brought before the council they again refused to take the oath and asserted their allegiance to the Catholic faith. Condemned to death, they were hanged for treason in 1535 at Tyburn. Humphrey Middlemore was beatified by Pope Leo XIII in 1886.

By an irony of history another Birmingham man was the first Protestant martyr under Queen Mary, the Catholic eldest daughter of Henry by Catherine of Aragon. He was John Rogers. Born and raised in Deritend and a worshipper at St John's in the village, Rogers went on to study at Cambridge and Oxford, where he espoused the cause of Protestantism. After two years as a vicar in London he went to Antwerp as chaplain to the Merchant Adventurers. William Tyndale was also in the city working on a translation of the Bible from Latin to English. Henry VIII was then a staunch Catholic and his agents captured Tyndale. Fetched back to England he was killed in 1536. Rogers completed and edited Tyndale's translation. It is called the Matthew Bible as Rogers used the pseudonym of Thomas Matthew to protect him. After Henry broke with Catholic Church this Bible, in 1537 he passed a proclamation for this Bible to be provided for all to read, in every parish of the land.

Rogers married and then ministered in Germany. In the reign of Edward VI, Henry's son, the marriage of priests was tolerated and Rogers returned to England and became a vicar in London. His situation became dangerous, however, when Mary took the throne. Rogers was called upon to preach publicly. He knew that his words would be harked at carefully. Undaunted, in his sermon Rogers denounced what he considered Papal errors and asserted Protestant beliefs. Eventually he was arrested and imprisoned for over a year, during which time his wife and ten children were not allowed to see him.

In 1555 Rogers was condemned for marrying though he was a priest and for not believing in the mass. When he was sentenced he explained that his poor wife was a German and a stranger in the land and he asked if she might be allowed to speak to him before he died. He was told that she was not his wife. Rogers replied that she was and had been for eighteen years. Offered a pardon if he would recant, answered defiantly: 'that which I have preached with my lips will I seal with my blood'. Soon afterwards he was taken out of jail to be burnt in Smithfield. Folk came out with candles to light his way and in the huge crowd he saw his wife and his ten children; the youngest was a baby. The French Ambassador wrote that Rogers went along as one who goes to a wedding. He and the Blessed Humphrey Middlemore had a devout belief and both were martyred for it.

The Middlemores of Edgbaston remained staunch Catholics. Both the Richard Middlemore who died in 1647 and his son, Robert, were Catholic recusants and had to pay the substantial fine of £100 a year for their loyalty. During the English Civil War, Richard took the part of the king – unsurprisingly as the Parliamentarians counted amongst their number those who hated Catholics. Unhappily in 1643 his residence of Edgbaston Hall was captured by Colonel John Fox, known as Tinker Fox of Walsall (see Tinkers Farm Road). He is supposed to have fortified and garrisoned it with 400 horse and foot. Then in June 1644 Fox was authorised to hold the mansion-house and manor of Edgbaston, and to receive the revenues payable to Middlemore in the parishes of Kings Norton, Yardley and Northfield.

As for Richard Middlemore, he was not passive. He fought at the siege of Hawkesley House later in 1643, when his distant kinsman, William Middlemore, was attacked by the parliamentary forces. Later that year Hawkesley was recaptured by the Royalists. Richard probably fought elsewhere for the king and was regarded as a 'delinquent'. He died in 1647. His son, Robert, survived him by five years. In turn Robert's son, Richard, died at the young age of 28 in about 1660. He left no heir and was succeeded by his aunt, Mary. She was married to Sir John Gage, another Catholic. He was a generous benefactor to the building of the Franciscan chapel at

Birmingham in 1687 (see Masshouse Lane). Mary and Sir John had two daughters, one of whom inherited Edgbaston. Named Bridget she married the third Viscount Fauconberg and in 1717 they sold Edgbaston to the Calthorpes.

Although the Edgbaston Middlemores had died out, two younger branches carried on: one was based at Hazelwell, Kings Norton (Kings Heath), and the other at Hawkesley, Northfield. William was the last of the Hazelwell Middlemores. He died in 1708. The Hawkesley Middlemores, however, carried on into the nineteenth century. Like the Middlemores of Edgbaston and Hazelwell, the Hawkesley family remained true to the Catholic faith and were Royalists in the Civil War – and suffered as a result. Hawkesley House ultimately descended to Richard Middlemore who died in 1831.

Arising from the Hawkesley Middlemores was a branch of the family in Birmingham. One of them, Richard, was appointed honorary surgeon to the Birmingham Eye Infirmary in 1835 and in 1843 was appointed surgeon to the Blind Asylum at Edgbaston. Then in 1888 he presented £1,000 to the Birmingham and Midland Eye Hospital for the post graduate lectures on ophthalmic practice He died in 1891.

His brother, William, became a wealthy and prominent citizen, through his success in building the family's saddlery and leather business. Radical in politics he was elected a town councillor and became one of the founders of the Birmingham Liberal Association in 1865 and of the Education League four years later. His own immediate ancestors had ceased to be Catholics and become Anglicans, but William himself was a Baptist. He gave generously to the building of Baptist chapels, and with his brothers Richard and James rebuilt the chancel of Edgbaston Parish Church. Unlike Josiah Mason he kept his philanthropy quiet, but was responsible for giving the recreation ground in Burbury Street to the City. This was thought to have cost £14,000.

One of William's sons also made a major mark upon Birmingham. He was John Throgmorton Middlemore. Born at Edgbaston in 1844 he was educated at the Edgbaston Proprietary School and went on to stay with his maternal uncle in America and to study medicine in Maine. During his four-year stay, the young Middlemore travelled widely in the Midwest and parts of eastern Canada. In particular he was impressed with the open spaces in Ontario, the apparent absence of class divisions, and the optimism about their lives of the local people.

Returning from America he was elected to the town council of Birmingham in 1883 and was returned M.P. for North Birmingham in 1899 as a Unionist. The giver of a fine collection of Burne-Jones paintings to the Art Gallery, perhaps he is best known, as the founder in 1872 of the Children's Emigration Home in Birmingham and the Middlemore Home at Halifax, Nova Scotia.

In 1872 Middlemore took over a house for boys on St Luke's Road and one for girls not far away in Spring Street. Seven years later purpose-built homes were opened in St Luke's Road with separate provision for boys and girls. Middlemore wanted to rescue children that were looked down upon as 'street urchins' from a bad family life, as he saw it. He felt that the back streets of Birmingham contrasted unfavourably with the open spaces of Canada; and he hoped that by taking 'street arabs' out of what he felt was an immoral setting that he could do something good.

Today many people might regard Middlemore's attitudes as patronising and overweening and feel that it was wrong to grab children from their homes and uproot them – but like many middle-class Victorian men he was certain in his beliefs and actions. He asserted that "children are not taken to Canada because they are poor, but to save them from their bad companions, to whom, if they remained in Birmingham, they would always be tempted to return. Emigration is the only mode of permanently separating these children from their old associations.'

Between 1873 and 1936 more than 5,000 young immigrants aged between two and eighteen were sent to Canada. Thereafter children were sent to Australia. Some of the youngsters did well, but others who were used as cheap labour and almost as slaves had hard and distressing times. This child emigration programme was one of a number, some of which were larger. However, it is unique in that many of its internal records are openly available on microfilm for family and social history studies, and the British Isles Family History Society of Greater Ottawa (BIFHSGO) has an important web site that provides resources for Middlemore researchers.

In 1919, John Throgmorton Middlemore was knighted as the first baronet of Selly Oak, for his services to his community. He died on 17 October 1924. Five years later, new homes were opened in Selly Oak. These were occupied until 1955 when the Middlemore Homes Committee sold them to Birmingham Council. They became Westhill College. Middlemore Road, Northfield recalls these Middlemore Homes and the Middlemore family who lived nearby at Hawkesley. Today the Middlemore Committee now supports families in need.

Much of the information in this section is mostly taken from W. P. W. Phillimore, *Some Account of the Family Middlemore* (1901).

Middleton Hall Road, Cotteridge and Kings Norton

Going from the heart of Cotteridge and the Pershore Road to Bunbury Road and thence Northfield Village, Middleton Hall Road recalls one of the two sub manors of Northfield. They were Selly, in existence at the time of Domesday in 1086; and Middleton, which was in existence by the late twelfth century when Ralph Paynell gave the land of Middletune and la Haie (**Hay Green Lane**, Bournville) to Bernard Paynell. Middleton means the middle estate and one hundred years later the manor was held by a family that took their name from their estate. This remained with the Middletons until the late fourteenth century, after which time it passed through the hands of various families. From about 1596 Middleton belonged to the Cookes family but manorial rights seem to have lapsed by 1813. Thereafter the only reminder of the manor was Middleton Hall Farm near to the boundaries with Kings Norton.

Milk Street, Deritend

Today Milk Street goes from High Street Deritend to the junction of Bordesley Street with Little Anne Street and thence becomes Barn Street. It is an old way that is shown on the first map of Birmingham by Westley in 1731 but is called Rope Walk on Bradford's Map of 1750. It then ran through fields but did not reach Deritend High Street, simply because of the development along that road; instead it ended at Moore's Row. Hansom's Map of 1778, however, introduces the name of Milk Street, but it remains in a rural setting – perhaps leading to a name associated with agriculture. Over the next few decades, Deritend and Digbeth became built over, but it was not until 1880 that a clearance of property led to Milk Street running from Moore's Row to Deritend High Street via what had been Meeting House Yard.

A rare photo of veterans from the First World War gathering in Milk Street by High Street Deritend and the 'Big Bull's Head' gathering to remember their fallen comrades, probably in the mid-1930s. They are members of the Digbeth Branch of the British Legion. The man on the left of the second row and wearing the flat cap is Henry Smith. His daughter, Freda Child, tells me that he was wearing the Mons Star amongst other medals. Henry was a founder member of the Digbeth Branch and became secretary and standard bearer. He was also a member of the Old Contemptibles. The Branch met first at Digbeth Institute and then in Dean Street, where it was the first and perhaps the only teetotal branch. After the Second World War it moved to Thorp Street Barracks. The man in the bowler hat on the right may be Sir Smedley Crooke, MP for Deritend and well known as a supporter of ex-servicemen. Thanks to Geoff Dowling.

Milk Street was one of the poorest parts of Birmingham in the late nineteenth and early twentieth centuries. In 1893, Dr Alfred Hill, the City's Medical Officer of Health, inspected the sanitary condition there and in and around Woodcock Street. His report could have applied to many other streets in the central area. None of the property was good. Back-to-back houses predominated and most had deteriorated roofs, floors, sinks, walls and wash-houses. Dampness was prevalent because of a lack of damp courses and leaky roofs and porous quarry tiles on the floor. The yards were unpaved and sodden with filth, the drainage and sewerage was bad, and the buildings were crowded together and badly arranged. The first house in Number One Court Milk Street was merely seven feet from other dwellings. Such circumstances meant that there was a lack of light and fresh air. Unsurprisingly, the awful environment was a danger to the health of the residents.

Two years later, Hill took a population census for the Milk Street neighbourhood. He estimated that its death rate was twice as high as the average for the city and recommended that the only remedy was for the whole district to be included in an improvement scheme that would allow a reconstruction of the streets and houses hereabouts. The Housing of the Working Classes Act (1890) allowed the council to prepare such a scheme outside Corporation Street (see Corporation Street) and in 1894 the Improvement Committee proposed to compulsorily purchase the buildings in those parts of Woodcock Street and Milk Street that were declared insanitary and then to demolish them and replace them with 116 new dwellings. Cost led to the dropping of the plans for Woodcock Street but in 1895 Parliament approved the plans for Milk Street.

Over the next two years, 65 homes and a few workshops were knocked down. They were replaced with four two-storey blocks of tenements. In total they held 61 homes of between two and four rooms. They were finished in 1900 and let at between 3s (15p) and 5s (25p) a week. This latter rent was too high for the poor, many of whom had to provided for families on an income of between 10s (50p) and 17s 6d (88p) a week. These flats were demolished in 1966. Today Milk Street is bereft of residents.

Mill Lane, Weoley Castle

Connecting Stonehouse Lane with Millmead Road, Mill Lane harks back to Connop's Mill that stood on the Stonehouse Brook. It was probably one of the mills of Northfield that was first mentioned in documents of the thirteenth century. It was marked in 1834 and was called Connop's Mill in 1873 after Benjamin Connop, who was a miller, farmer, and beer retailer; and it later became the Mill Inn and Mill Farm. The buildings disappeared during the building of the Weoley Castle housing estate.

Millpool Hill, Kings Heath

That section of the Alcester Road South between Broad Lane and Limekiln Lane, Millpool Hill rises above the valley of the Chinn Brook. It dates back to the eighteenth century and a Mill Pool Hill Farm stood in the neighbourhood of the modern Meadfoot Avenue. However, neither the mill nor its pool have been located. **Limekiln Lane** was once part of Millpool Hill.

Moat Lane, Bull Ring

Buildings not people dominate the modern Bull Ring. Buildings such as Selfridge's, an icon of twenty-first century Birmingham, overlooked only by the Rotunda, a symbol of 1960s Birmingham. Between them lie a host of new structures that call out that this is a go-ahead city that looks only forward and never glances back. But here and there the past whispers to us and asks us to turn our heads if only for a moment to glimpse our history.

Our parish church, the true and everlasting heart of our city, speaks poignantly and persuasively of all those that came before. Its chantries and monuments, memorials and stained glass windows, gravestones and bells all bid us be still to hark at the voices of those long gone. Those voices are strengthened by a clutch of nearby street names that tantalisingly talk to us of those that once were – if we but listen. Mill Lane where stood a mill. Dean Street where perhaps a tragic fellow called John a Dean drowned in a stream that flowed where now traffic only flows. The Bull Ring where bulls were tied to a ring on a wall and then baited by dogs. And Moat Lane, recalling a moat that did encircle a manor house.

That's a building that you would not expect in the middle of Birmingham, a moated manor house. Baddesley Clinton in Warwickshire, Harvington Hall in Worcestershire, and Stokesay Castle in Shropshire – they are all where you would expect to find a moated manor house, in the midst of beautiful English countryside. There then is the historical clue, Birmingham too was once embraced by the countryside and its lords also lived in a manor house that was protected by a moat.

The first notice we get of such a building is in the charter granted in 1166 by Henry II for Peter de Birmingham and his heirs to hold a market 'at his castle of Birmingham'. It is likely that this was a ringwork, whereby a hall and other buildings were enclosed by a bank, fence and ditch that was perhaps water-filled and which was approached by a fortified entrance. Little archaeological evidence of this 'castle' came to light in the excavations carried out before the redevelopment of the latest Bull Ring shopping centre, but it suggest that the manor house was a stone building with moulded stonework.

In the second charter granted by Richard I to William de Bermingham in 1189 there is no mention of a castle. Instead reference is made to William's house, perhaps indicating the building of a manor house protected by a proper moat. Excavations indicate that the old manor house was replaced by another stone building in the thirteenth century. Mike Hodder, Birmingham's Archaeologist, feels that this manor house would have looked similar to Weoley Castle, with stone and timber buildings. In this house, the descendants of Peter lived until the decline and fall of the de Bermingham family.

The last of their name to be Lord of Birmingham was Edward. Apparently he did not live in the old manor house because in 1529 a survey of Birmingham indicated that it had fallen into disrepair: 'the Manor House is moted rounde aboute and hath

An atmospheric photo of Moat Lane taken in 1957. Market traffic blocks passage to all except those on foot, like the porter who heads up towards Saint Martin's and Spiceal Street, the home of Brum's barrow boys and flower sellers until they were pushed from their historical pitches for the 1960s redevelopment of the Bull Ring. On the left is the wholesale fruit and vegetable market, and across the way are the places of business of George Jackson, the Talbot public house, Glover and Burley fruit salesmen and Francis Nicholls fruit merchants.

a drawebrygge to the same, and the mote ys sore o'r growen w't wede and Fulle of Mudde and Ash Robussh, and the most pte of the Manor place Fallen downe, and the Resydew that standyth ys sore decayed so that no man wyll hyre hit'. Edward fell foul either of the machinations of more powerful men or of his own stupidity in meddling in the affairs of such people. Whatever the case, he was sent to the Tower of London and in 1536 his manor was taken from him and given to the King by act of Parliament. His family home went into decay.

No more is heard of the moat until the first map of Birmingham by William Westley in 1731. Moat Lane is shown as running from opposite the parish church in Saint Martin's Lane and down along the ancient seat of the Lord Birmingham' and into fields. The map includes drawings, one of which is of the moat surrounding buildings that lie to the west of Moat Lane.

By the time of William Hutton, Birmingham's first historian, the site of the manor house was simply called The Moat. In 1783, he explained that it was 'situated about sixty yards south of the church, and twenty west of Digbeth'. The moat itself was circular 'and supplied by a small stream that crosses the road to Bromsgrove, near the first mile stone'. This stream originally ran into the River Rea, 'near Vaughton's hole, dividing the parishes of Birmingham and Edgbaston all the way; but at the formation of the Moat, it was diverted from its course, into which it never returned'.

In his expressive way, Hutton described how 'the old castle followed its lords, and is buried in the ruins of time.' The moat itself 'being filled with water, has nearly the same appearance now as perhaps a thousand years ago, but not altogether the same use. It then served to protect its master, but now to turn a thread-mill.' As for the manor house it had been replaced by one 'in the modern style' occupied by a manufacturer. This Moat House had been advertised for sale on 4 January 1765. It contained four rooms on each of its three floors and had a large back kitchen, convenient warehouses and workshops, and other buildings. The whole could be converted into a manufactory capable of employing 300 people.

Five years later in *The Street and Inhabitants of Birmingham* by Sketchley and Adams, the first trades directory for Birmingham, the Moat House was occupied by Francis and Ashton, nail factors. Moat Lane was mentioned; although it had also been known as Court Lane from the outer court of the manor house and in which the Moat mill was found. The directory also mentioned a street just called Moat – perhaps **Moat Row**, which is named as such on Hanson's map of 1778.

Though in decay, the moat itself could still present a danger. Ten years later, a man driving a one-horse chaise got 'too near the edge of the water, the ground gave way, when the chaise, man, and horse were all overturned into the moat. It was with great difficulty that either the man or the horse were saved; and as people are frequently falling into this water, it now becomes absolutely necessary that the rotten bank should be repaired, and some kind of railing erected.'

Near to the moat were Bagnes Meadows, where horses and cows grazed as late as 1791, but within a few years the last traces both of the de Bermingham's manor house and the rural Bull Ring were banished. In 1812, the Street Commissioners, then Birmingham's ruling body, decided as Hutton bemoaned 'to destroy every vestige of the habitation of our ancient lords, by taking down the buildings, filling up the moat, and laying the whole open as a market'.

The site was covered with the Smithfield Market for wholesale fruit and vegetables, which was opened in 1817. John Alfred Langford, another early historian of our city, alerted his readers to the swift transformation of the centre of Birmingham. Where the House of the Birminghams had stood surrounded by its defensive and dangerous moat the neighbourhood was now 'thronged with a busy and energetic people, whose incessant traffic renders the idea of a blade of grass growing there wilder than the wildest fancy of the poet'.

Moat Lane is still thronged with incessant traffic, much of which is parked in a drab multi-storey that stands on the site of the old manor house; but in its name at least, Moat Lane catches hold of at quieter days when Birmingham was but a small market town enclosed by the countryside.

Moilliet Street, Winson Green

Coming off the Dudley Road, this street highlights a Swiss family that was of influence in early to mid-nineteenth Birmingham and Smethwick. In the 1790s Jean-Louis Moilliet came from a place near to Geneva and arrived at Soho House, the home of Matthew Boulton, with a letter of introduction and credit of £10,000. It was a fabulous sum. Through Boulton introduced Moilliet met James Keir, a chemist, industrialist and member of the Lunar Society, and Keir's only child, Amelia. In 1801 she married Moilliet at All Saint's Church, West Bromwich. He became a naturalised citizen and changed his name to John Lewis Moilliet. The couple lived in a house in Newhall Street, at the back of which was a warehouse in which Moilliet operated as a continental merchant. This firm became Moilliet and Gem and moved to extensive premises in Charlotte Street. Moilliet also founded a bank which amalgamated with Lloyd's Bank in the mid-nineteenth century.

In 1813 he bought Smethwick Grove and its sixteen-acre estate near the eastern boundary of Smethwick on the east side of what is now Grove Lane. Over the next few years he bought more land, especially from Piddocks Farm, and by 1828 owned 59 acres. That year he also purchased the short stretch of the old line of the Birmingham Canal which ran through his estate and made an ornamental pool. By that date Moilliet and his family had moved to Hamstead Hall in Handsworth and the Grove was let to George Bacchus, a partner in a Birmingham firm of flint-glass manufacturers (see Bacchus Road). The Moilliets son, James, then moved into the house in 1832 after his marriage to Lucy Harriet Galton of the gunmaking and banking Quaker family (see Farmer Street).

Amelia Moilliet was great friends with Maria Edgeworth, She was the daughter of Richard Lovell Edgeworth, an inventor, educator and reformer who was another member of the Lunar Society and whose family were landowners in Ireland. Maria became a well-known novelist and wrote regularly to Amelia. She liked John Moilliet, describing him as 'intelligent without pretension', and was impressed by the family's mode of life which was 'mercantile and literary and domestic'. Amelia Moilliet herself kept a diary between 1819 and 1828. It is filled with information about trips to Geneva and elsewhere, visitors to Smethwick Grove and support for the anti-slavery movement and other good causes.

In 1844 the Moilliets moved to Abberley Hall in Worcestershire. John Lewis died the next year and was succeeded as Lord of the Manor by his son, James. **Abberley Street** runs at the bottom of Moilliet Street and recalls the lordship.

Moland Street, Gosta Green

Now a rump of a street coming off Bagot Street, itself running from the start of New Town Row, Moland Street brings to mind a family that was mentioned in an abstract of title of Moland family for an estate in the parish of Aston between 1668-1799. Moland Street is mentioned in documents dating to 1809-17 and in an act enabling Richard Moland, the 'natural guardian of his infant daughters Elizabeth, Anna Maria, Loetitia Martha and Margaret Lucy during their minorities to grant building leases of one undivided moiety of their lands in Birmingham and Aston'.

Monument Road, Ladywood and Edgbaston

It is hard to think that the busy Monument Road was once the setting for a romance but so it is. The story goes that once a wealthy young man apparently built a tower from which he could espy his lady-love who lived in Aston a few miles to the east. Well a tower was built but for what purpose is not known. Today it is called Perrot's Folly and it is regarded by some as Birmingham's oddest architectural feature. At 96 feet in height and boasting seven storeys, the brick tower was built in 1758 by John Perrot, hence **Perrott Street**, Winson Green. He came from Belbroughton, Worcestershire but went on to live at the Lodge (see Lodge Road). His grandfather Humphrey had bought Rotton Park from Sir Edward Marrow, the Lord of the Manor of Birmingham, in1628. At that time Rotton Park included much of Ladywood and Birmingham Heath, and it had been the hunting ground of the de Berminghams.

Another story explains that John Perrot put up the tower not see the woman he craved but to look at the grave of his wife ten miles away in Belbroughton – but the Clent Hills blocked out the view, however, hence his tower was a folly. More realistically, Drake in his *Picture of Birmingham* (1825) believed that the monument was built for an observatory; although Showell in his Dictionary of Birmingham stated that Perrot was a keen courser and stood in the tower so that he might watch the hunting. Whatever the case, the building led to Icknield Street West becoming Monument Lane and then Monument Road in 1878.

Perceptively, Drake also observed that although the monument was 'subservient to no direct purpose of utility, it forms, as seen from the reservoir, &c, a beautiful feature in the landscape, and we cannot altogether coincide in the propriety of the

A cracking shot of the 'Duke of Wellington' pub on the corner of Monument Road and Leach Street, which was surrounded on three sides by Icknield Square. Taken in 1959 it also shows John Marshall, the hairdresser; Swift's Shoes; Cyril Slaughter, grocer; Watty's, the fishing tackle dealer; and George Baines George, the baker's.

title—*Perrot's Folly*—by which it is not unfrequently designated'. This seems more likely and it may also be that Perrot also saw the tower as a place where he could entertain friends in remarkable surroundings and observe the countryside.

He died aged 74 and the Folly passed to his only surviving daughter, Catherine Noel – thus **Noel Road**, Edgbaston. Her son was John Perrot-Noel and he sold the Folly gradually. Joseph Gillott bought a large part of it in 1849 for £100,000 (see Gillott Road); and another buyer was an iron merchant called William Henry Stewart, hence **Stewart Street**, Spring Hill. Interestingly, though, Perrot's Folly did come to have an importance as an observatory after it was leased as such by Follet Osler in 1884 (see Osler Street). It was one of the world's first weather forecasting centres and, as Edgbaston Observatory, was in use as until 1979.

During the inter-war years it was presided over by Mr Kelly whose weather predictions often appeared in the *Birmingham Mail*. Gordon K. Wright now lives in Weston super Mare but grew up in Reservoir Road, Edgbaston. He remembers that he 'once had the great pleasure of meeting Mr Kelly and climbing to the top of the folly itself, where I recall a magnificent view of all the Edgbaston I knew and many more miles as well'.

Gordon emphasises that it is not the only tower in **Waterworks Road** as each day on his way to Saint George's School in Plough and Harrow Road he passed the waterworks tower, although he and his pals never thought it...

to be a chimney as we observed through the glass windows some large structure of metal going up and down and making a thumping noise. The thump could be heard throughout the neighbourhood all day and night. Before the offices were built on the south side there was a large field with hundreds of very large black pipes which was an ideal playground for us children, many a sneak ten minutes was ours to create adventure amongst the pipes until some official spotted us, then it was a beeline for our escape route through the fence 'known only to a few'.

Many a happy adventure was ours until they commenced to build the massive office block that still is there today, whenever I visit. But now came another episode of adventure, with the builders came steel girders and cranes, hundreds of them and months of building from the ground up, although there was a rather fierce looking watchman on guard day and night, we still had good healthy fun amongst the girders and the cranes but with building came the eventual blocking out of our seeing the gang at the 'waterworks' after school.

Now operated by Severn Trent, this waterworks tower once belonged to the City of Birmingham Waterworks Department. Built in 1862 it is a beautiful Italianate structure that is reminiscent of a Lord's tower in Renaissance Italy.

Many readers regard these two towers as the inspiration behind the Twin Towers in Tolkien's *Lord of the Rings*. In 1902, Tolkien went with his mother, Mabel, and brother from their home in Kings Heath to Oliver Road, Edgbaston. Mabel had converted to Catholicism and their new home was near to where she worshipped at the Oratory on the Hagley Road. After a spell in Rednal (see Lickey Road), where Mabel sadly died, the boys moved back to live with their mother's sister in Stirling Road, Edgbaston. Living across the way was Dr Joseph Sampson Gamgee, a doctor who founded the Birmingham Hospital Fund, whose headquarters are at Gamgee House, just off Monument Road. He also lives on in the person of Sam Gamgee, the most loyal and resolute companion of Frodo Baggins in the *Lord of the Rings*.

Monyhull Hall Road, Kings Norton

This long road going from Brandwood Road to Parsons Hill was formerly Branderd Lane Road, which meant burnt wood (see Brandwood Road), and it has nothing to do with money nor with many; rather Monyhull is derived from the Anglo-Saxon Mannan-hylls, meaning Mann's hill. For hundred of years, the people of the west midlands have turned an 'a' before an 'n' or 'm' into an 'o', hence 'Mom' and 'Mon' for 'Man'. In this case Mannan was pronounced Monnan-hyll, and indeed the first recorded reference from 1237 is written as Monhull; and by the sixteenth century it was Monyhull.

A separate manor within Kings Norton, Monyhull had a watermill on the Chinn Brook from 1286. It was later was held by the College of Westbury, Gloucestershire, but after Henry VIII dissolved the monasteries and other religious bodies, it seems to have gone the Sparry family. Avowed Catholics, the Sparrys were bowed down by fines for clinging to their faith and had to sell in 1610 to William Child. Two years before, we get the first mention of Monyhull Hall, although tree ring dating of its roof timbers have showed that the roof timbers were put up between 1466 and 1501 – making it the same age as the 'Old Crown' in Deritend. The hall was rebuilt in the 1730s and additions were made in the nineteenth century.

In 1864 the hall and its 128 acre estate was sold to Ezra Milward, a gun manufacturer; and in 1905 it was purchased by the Birmingham, Aston and Kings Norton Joint Poor Law Establishment 'for the purpose of the provision and maintenance of Homes for the reception and treatment of sane epileptics and feeble-minded persons'. This was regarded as a bold move, but the eugenicist language of the time dismissed the humanity of those who came to live at what was called the Monyhull Colony. Fortunately their dignity, pride and intelligence have been brought to the fore in a caring book by Deborah Hutchings called *Monyhull 1908-1998. A History of Caring*. One of those who lived at Monyhull was Lily Miles. She was there for 65 years and had left home with a breaking heart and bitter tears. She tried to bear her lot with content and appealed passionately, 'Oh dear friends, forget me not'.

Moor Street, City

Pebble Mill Road, Edgbaston; Thimblemill Lane, Nechells; Hawkesley Mill Lane, Northfield; Duddeston Mill Road, Duddeston; Miller Street, Aston; Heath Mill Lane, Deritend; Mill Street, Sutton Coldfield and Mill Street by Dartmouth Circus; Millpool Hill, Alcester Lane's End; Mill Road, Hay Mills; Mill Lane, Bartley Green– all are expressive street names that pull us into the pools and waters of the mills which abounded in what is now Birmingham. More than 70 mills once stood on the waterways of the rivers Rea, Tame, and Cole, and the brooks Hawthorn, Hockley, Aston, Hol, Plants, Bourn, Stonehouse, and Chinn. All of them bar Sarehole Mill and Newhall Mill have gone, but their impact on our history should not be dismissed for mills played a significant role in the development of Birmingham from 1166.

In the villages and towns of Medieval England, mills for the grinding of corn were vital for the well being both of the local economy and community. Birmingham was no exception and there was a mill that stood in the outer court of the manor house of the de Bermingham family in what was to become the Bull Ring. It was driven by the outflow of the moat that protected this building – hence it was known as the Moat Mill or the Malt Mill; whilst the moat itself and its pool were filled by water from the Lady Well (now beneath The Arcadian) and from 'a clear water stream from Edgbaston'.

Giving its name to **Upper Mill Lane**, now little more than a passageway just below St Martin's, the Moat Mill was held by Elizabeth Bermingham, the widow of Edward, who was the last of his family to hold the manor after which it was named.

A superb pair of 'before and after' photos. The first shows Moor Street and the corner with Carrs Lane in the 1950s. The large whitish building in the background is the old Market Hall. A decade later all these buildings from the 'Corner' pub down towards the Bull Ring have been demolished for the building of the Inner Ring Road, along with two long-established, short and narrow streets – Scotland Passage and Castle Street. They would have been in the land that has been cleared between the policeman and the large buildings in the background of the photograph opposite.

After her death in 1559, her third husband, William Askerick, became the tenant. About ten years before he had built a new corn mill and pool on the stream that ran down from the Moat to the River Rea. It was also powered by a diversion of the River Rea. This Town Mill, as it was called, led to the name of Lower Mill Lane. Now called just **Mill Lane** it is above Digbeth Coach Station, but for many years it was also referred to as **Tan Row**. This was because in the sixteenth century the Tan Yard of the Elesmere family was found alongside the stream from the Moat, and in which they washed the skins of animals before tanning them into hide.

Eventually the Town Mill was taken over by Robert Porter, who converted it into a blade mill. During the English Civil War it was believed that Porter turned out swords for the Parliamentarian forces and in 1643 it was destroyed by Prince Rupert's men when he led a force of Royalists in sacking Birmingham. Later rebuilt

The officer is stopping traffic coming up the Bull Ring into High Street, and a sign is telling motorists to turn right for Dale End and Albert Street. Behind the policeman is a sign for Bryant's Builders, one of the most important in the rebuilding of post-war Birmingham, and to his right are two children who are walking by the railings that surrounded Nelson's Statue. On the right, the large building is the Moor Street Warehouse, in front of which is Moor Street Station – the only structure which still stands following yet another development of the city centre in the early twenty-first century.

as a corn mill, The Town Mill became a slitting mill in the eighteenth century and stayed as such until the early 1800s, when it was changed back to a corn mill. It seems to have disappeared by the mid-nineteenth century and from 1897 the site was probably occupied by the Meat Market.

The Malt Mill was also changed into industrial use. In 1712 it was described as the Moat blade mill. Afterwards used as a thread mill, it was cleared for the building of the Smithfield Market, opened in 1817. Both the Town Mill and Moat Mill stood upon the slopes of the Rea Valley; by contrast the Heath Mill was on the banks of the river. Lying across Deritend Bridge and at the top end of **Heath Mill Lane**, it may have been there from the fifteenth century, but certainly it is mentioned in a lease from 1526. From the late 1600s, this corn mill was in the tenancy of the Cooper family and it was they who transformed it into a blade mill in the mid-1700s.

By the early 19th century, it was named Deritend Forge or Woolley's Mill, after James Woolley, who was a sword cutler. Like the Town Mill, its use reverted to the grinding of corn and it seems then to have become part of local factories.

So three street names in the old manor of Birmingham hark back to mills – so, too, does Moor Street, according to some. It is said that Moor is a corruption of Molle and that this word itself is derived from the French word 'moulin', meaning a mill. Accordingly it is supposed that there had been a mill in Moor Street. Another interpretation is that Moor Street was connected with the family of Roger le Moule mentioned in a document in 1310. Whatever its origins, Moor Street is crucial for understanding the history of Birmingham. In the excavations that preceded the construction of the latest Bull Ring shopping centre, shards of Roman pottery were found at digs in Moor Street and Park Street. Mike Hodder, the City Archaeologist, feels that this small but significant quantity hints at a farmstead hereabouts.

Nothing was found from the Anglo-Saxon period, but importantly the archaeologists came across evidence for the early years of the new town of Birmingham that had been founded in 1166. Foremost was a massive ditch that was almost five yards wide and two yards deep. It ran from about a third of the way along Moor Street down to Park Street and would seem to have been a watercourse and a boundary. To the west of the ditch were the back plots of the houses that fronted on to the Bull Ring; and to the east was the Little or Over Park of the Lord of the Manor. Fascinatingly, samples of plants and pollen from the early 1200s confirm the presence of parkland and woodland, or at least firewood and tanning bark brought in to the town; whilst cereals from the late thirteenth century suggest animal fodder and the keeping of livestock in the back plots.

The ditch soon fell into disuse and became a big miskin. Pits were then dug into it, which were also filled with rubbish. One contained charcoal and shards of pottery that were badly burned – and interestingly there is a reference to a great fire in Birmingham in about 1300. A sliver of a crucible, debris from the hammering of a hot iron, and fragments of coal were also found, intimating at the emergence of industrial activity.

It seems that the filling in of the ditch was followed by the cutting of Moor Street and Park Street. People wanted to come and live in an expanding market town and there was a need for fresh plots to be laid out for them in new streets. Both streets seem to have emerged by the end of the thirteenth century, or at least by the early fourteenth century, and soon became established streets so that by 1437 a lease of a tenement and land in 'Mowlestrete' was granted by John Belle, master of the Gild of the Holy Cross in Birmingham and brethren and sisters of the same, to John Crowe of Birmingham. When the name changed from Moule or Mowle Street to Moor Street is not known but another lease of 1684 mentions 'Mole alias Moore Street', as do documents from 1715 and 1738. However in a deed from 1748 it is given merely as Moor Street.

Watercourses were essential for the new burgesses of Birmingham. One was called Hersum's (meaning Lord's) or Hassam's Ditch, which appears in deeds relating to Moor Street from 1341 to 1681. It ran alongside the 'Woolpack Hotel', which is supposed to have replaced an older inn called the 'Green Tree'. In the middle years of the eighteenth century, the 'Woolpack' was a favourite haunt of John Baskerville, the famed printer, and others who believed in bringing about a reform of Parliament. Along with other prominent citizens, he also lived for a time in Moor Street – as had done William Lench, the founder of Lench's Trust (see Lench Street), the Colmores, the Smallbrooks and others in the past.

The houses in the street were substantial. In 1772 a sale described one as 'a large commodious dwelling house', having two malt houses, an entire yard, stable and garden. Moor Street also boasted the 'White Horse', the headquarters of the Warwickshire Militia, and the Playhouse. Built as a theatre in about 1740, it was later rented by followers of the charismatic preacher John Wesley – who opened it as such in 1764.

In the early years of the nineteenth century the Birmingham Public Office and prison was erected in Moor Street. Greatly extended in 1830 and again 35 years later, the various structures of the Public Office acted as the centre of local government before the opening of the Council House in 1879. The subsequent move of the municipal dignitaries signalled the future redundancy of the Public Office as well as the shifting of the official centre of Birmingham up the hill and away from the Bull Ring.

From 1909 much of the site of the Public Offices was covered in a Great Western Railway terminus. Five years later a permanent station was opened. It had an island platform of about 700 feet in length and two 100 feed long engine traversers. These did away with the need for a cross-over road and so economised on platform room. In addition, Moor Street Station had ample goods accommodation and it immediately became crucial to the successful running of Birmingham's markets. Previously fruit, vegetables, fish and meat had been delivered to the Hockley Goods Station, two miles distant, but now these supplies arrived right on the edge of the markets' complex.

The Station was one of the few buildings to survive the radical alteration of Moor Street in the redevelopment of the 1960s. Now superbly refurbished and proud in yet another new Bull Ring, its name encourages us to delve deep into a Birmingham that has gone.

Moor Green Lane, Moseley

This still winds its way like a country lane down from the Alcester Road, round Highbury Park and into Dogpool Lane. First mentioned in about 1250, moor means boggy land and green a fertile spot. However it may be that rather than taking its name from the landscape, Moor Green Lane recalls the Moore family. A mill once stood just above the point where Holders Lane reaches the River Rea. Known as Farmon's Mill or Moir Green Mill, it was a blade mill and was bought from John Middlemore by the Moores in 1597. They held it until 1783 when it was sold by John Moore to James Taylor of Moseley Hall. The Serjeant family leased the mill between

A tremendous photo of Moor Green Lane in 1932. The semi-detached houses in the background have been newly built and epitomise the modern world, but the carter and his horse hark back to an older, agricultural world in the throes of destruction.

1780 and 1841, and William Serjeant greatly improved the mill, then still a blade mill, between 1816 and 1841, after which it was bought by Charles Umpage, metal-roller. It was still in use as a rolling mill in the 1880s but soon after fell into disuse.

Moorsom Street, Newtown

Going between New Town Row and Elkington Street, this was called Harding Street until 1886. It may have been renamed because of the Aston Riots that took place two years before. From 1873 when he became mayor of Birmingham, Joseph Chamberlain and his Liberal supporters dominated the political affairs of Birmingham and nearby towns. The Conservatives were determined to change this and made a big push locally in the approach to the 1884 election. On 13 October that year they held a big rally in the Aston Lower Grounds, later Villa Park. Fearful of trouble, the local Conservatives hired 'roughs' to act as stewards. Some of the grass-roots Liberal leadership were outraged that the Conservatives were taking them on in their stronghold. Determined to confront their rivals they went round the back streets drawing in gang leaders to turn up with their followers and disrupt the meeting. The rally turned into a riot and Winston Churchill, then a popular Conservative, and Lord Northcote had to be saved from the fury of the mob. Ironically, Chamberlain was soon to split with the Liberals over the issue of Home Rule for Ireland. He formed a new party, the Liberal Unionists, which gradually merged with the Conservatives in Birmingham.

One of the gangs gained notoriety in the House of Commons as one of the worst involved in the riot. This was the Harding Street gang. Whether or not their actions led to the renaming of their street, it came to be called after C.R. Moorsom, who had been secretary of the London to Birmingham Railway Company in the late 1830s and early 1840s and who, as Captain Moorsom, was in command of the special constables during the Chartist Riots of 1848 in the Bull Ring (see Chartist Road).

Moors Row, Deritend

The connection between Milk Street and Floodgate Street, Moors Row now runs at the back of the old Floodgate Street School (later St Michael's Catholic School). Shown on Hanson's Map of 1778, Joe McKenna feels that because it is a low-lying spot close to the River Rea it would have been boggy and like a moor. However, in his fascinating book on the Folklore of Warwickshire (new edition 2004) Roy Palmer gives a more gripping account of its naming.

Tom Langley was a policeman who was first stationed in Digbeth in 1927. One night just after midnight, he was walking in Fazeley Street talking to the sergeant when they heard a terrible and spine-chilling scream from the direction of Milk Street. It crescendoed for some seconds and stopped suddenly. Tom thought someone had been called but the old sergeant stood still saying it was a sound that he would hear again, and although it might be put down to an engine 'some of the old Brums round here say it's a ghost but we are paid to catch thieves and not ghosts'.

Hearing the sound again two years later, Tom made enquiries. His uncle had served locally and had also been shaken by the sound but said it was best to forget it. Unable to do so, Tom chatted with a former policeman who was now a night watchman at a factory in Allison Street. His father had also been in the force in the district and he recounted an old story. When Prince Rupert sacked Birmingham in 1643, many of the people of the town had fled to the fields of Edgbaston and Winson Heath. One man named Moore did not. He stayed with his wife and five children in a cottage in Milk Street. Three of Rupert's men dragged the Moores into the street and beheaded all of them. The last to be murdered was a girl of thirteen. After seeing the vile deeds she screamed before she was slaughtered. The night watchman felt that her last terrible cry was still echoing down the years.

Moseley Road, Highgate and Balsall Heath

The Moseley Road is that stretch of the old road to Alcester that goes between Bradford Street and Edgbaston Road (to the west) and Trafalgar Road (to the east), which form the border between Balsall Heath with Moseley itself. In his ground-breaking article in *Midland History* on 'Birmingham before the Bull Ring', Steve Bassett suggests that the road from Alcester probably followed a pre-historic ridgeway – a long-distance route that dated back well before the Romans arrived in Britain and which kept to the high ground wherever possible. This was to avoid low-lying land that could be flooded and to ensure that the traveller had a vantage point from which to keep an eye out for danger from men or animals.

Even today on its course from the Camp Hill neighbourhood and as it follows the ridge above the River Rea, the road does rise markedly even though it falls back again here and there. At the junction with Edward Road the altitude is 425.5 feet, going up to 516 feet near Woodbridge Road, Moseley and to 526 feet at 'the Knob', the 'King's Arms' pub at Brandwood End. Despite the mass of buildings that envelop the Moseley Road today, wide views still open up in the Balsall Heath section down across the river valley and across to Edgbaston and the University of Birmingham. Those prospects were more spectacular in the early 1800s. The Georgian houses that are opposite Highgate Park and between Bradford Street and Stratford Place were built in the early nineteenth century and were advertised as having wonderful views of the Bromsgrove Lickey Hills. In 1818, the following description was given in Pye's *Directory of Modern Birmingham*:

> You leave Birmingham, either through Alcester-street or up Camphill,
> where there is a half-timbered house, inhabited by Mr. John Simcox, an
> attorney. a field nearly opposite there is perhaps the best view
> over the town of Birmingham that can be taken. A short distance
> beyond, on the right, is a row of houses, to which is given the name
> of Highgate. A little farther, on the left, is a tan-yard, upon an
> extensive scale, the property of Mr. Avery Homer.

In a field near the two mile stone, there is a grand panoramic view of
Birmingham, and the adjacent country for several miles on each side of
it, which is seen to the greatest advantage in an afternoon.

I recall that at one of my talks on the history of Birmingham I commented that such
a prospect would be impossible today but a chap told me that I was wrong. He used
to work at Robinson's Removals by Edgbaston Road (which building has now been
converted to apartments) and stated that from the upper levels there were fine views
of the Lickeys.

The ancient way from Alcester was like all ridgeways, it only crossed rivers when
it was unavoidable to do so. Today we tend to presume that all routes to Birmingham
crossed the River Rea between Deritend and Digbeth; however this may not have
been so. The modern line of the Moseley Road shows that as it approaches Camp
Hill, there is a pronounced shift to the north west. This was caused by the need to
avoid the Ravenshurst Estate of Mr Lowe, hence **Ravenhurst Street** and **Lowe
Street**, which was still farmland in the years immediately following the Napoleonic
Wars (see **Camp Hill**). The Moseley Road then runs into Bradford Street, down
which travellers could have gone towards the Digbeth crossing of the Rea and
Birmingham. However, Bradford Street itself was not cut out until 1767, when Henry
Bradford began to develop the Warner Fields Estate (see Bradford Street). Warner
Street also emerged and is the continuation of the Moseley Road across Bradford
Street and into Camp Hill and High Street Bordesley, which again gives access to the
crossing of the Rea at Digbeth.

Given that Bradford Street and Warner Street could not be used until at least the
mid-eighteenth century, then the old road from Alcester must have shifted not to the
north west to avoid the Ravenhurst Estate but to the south east. In this manner it may
have followed the old line of Stratford Place and along what is now the modern
Highgate Middleway. This old way would probably have gone across the road from
Stratford (see Stratford Road) and then down Sandy Lane, Watery Lane and Lawley
Street to cross the Rea at Duddeston. There is another possibility. This is that in ancient
times and through to the Middle Ages the way from Alcester did not have to divert to
avoid the Ravenhurst Estate. Instead it may have gone straight on, as is indicated on a
map drawn up for Henry Bradford in 1748. If this straight line is followed, it would
have gone across High Street Bordesley and directly to the ford at Duddeston, where
Lawley Middleway now goes under the railway viaducts. The Alcester Road would
then have joined the main route to Lichfield (see Lichfield Road).

There is no indication as to when the Alcester Road in Balsall Heath and Moseley
was named the Moseley Road, but it is given as such on the Earl of Dartmouth's Map
of 1823. It would be seem that the change came about because of the emergence of
Moseley as a distinct village around the Green. By that date there were still few
buildings on the Moseley Road. The 'Orange Tree' tavern stood where the Highgate
Fire Station now is and there was a large house with a tan yard on the site of modern

Looking along the Moseley Road from Camp Hill Station. Highgate Road is to the right and Belgrave Road to the left. Together they formed the boundary between Birmingham, Warwickshire and Kings Norton, Worcestershire, into which parish fell Balsall Heath until 1862. Montpellier Street lies between the two lamp posts on the right and the 'Orange Tree' would be on the left behind the shops that are close to the road.

In 1851 an Improvement Act was passed which established 'a united, complete and unfettered system of local government based upon the will of the inhabitants themselves', according to John Thackray Bunce in his *History of the Corporation* (Volume 1). This act transferred to the Corporation all the powers previously exercised by other local governing bodies and gave the Council complete authority over roads, sewers, lighting and sanitation. Other powers included those relating to street improvements and the removal of turnpike gates within the borough. A turnpike was a road administered by a trust and authorised by a private act of Parliament. The name came from a gate across the road that had a pike that formed a barrier to traffic and that was turned to allow access. These turnpike trusts were empowered to levy tolls on travellers at their gates. The money raised was spent on the upkeep and maintenance of the route, involving the digging of drainage ditches and the laying down a surface of stones and cinders.

The Alcester turnpike had a gate at Highgate (see Highgate Road) called the Bordesley Gate. This photo shows no sign of such a gate and hence must have been taken after 1851, when the Council took it down. Within the old parish of Birmingham, roads were macadamised before 1863 and thereafter many were made of Rowley Rag, stone from the Rowley hills. There is no sign of any macadam on the Moseley Road in this photo. As for footpaths, in the central area they consisted of round pebbles or small boulders that were difficult to walk upon and which were slowly replaced with flagging or asphalt in the main thoroughfares and Rowley Rag and blue bricks in the second-rate streets. In the suburbs the footpaths were made of gravel, which gave way to tar mixed with finely-broken stone and gravel. Interestingly, this photo indicates that the footpath heading into Birmingham was made whilst that on the Balsall Heath side was unmade. Consequently it would seem likely that this photo was taken in the late 1860s or early 1870s.

Lime Grove, which was owned by the Homer family (see Homer Street). Development along the Moseley Road in Balsall Heath, the stretch that begins at the junction with the Highgate Road and Belgrave Middleway, began to speed up from the 1830s, however. This urbanisation was further accelerated by the opening of Camp Hill Railway Station in 1840, followed six years later by the running of trams along the Moseley Road.

The growth of population encouraged the building of facilities, such as Saint Paul's Anglican Church on the corner of Saint Paul's Road and the Moseley Road in 1853, and it led to a demand from local people for Balsall Heath to separate itself from the rural Kings Norton. Thus in 1862 the district became a Local Board of Health. Thereafter, the Moseley Road developed as a civic centre. A Congregational Church with two eye-catching spires opened in the same year. It was followed a decade later by a Methodist Church, and in 1883 by the grand Moseley and Balsall Institute (see Institute Road).

In 1891 the Balsall Local Board of Health was taken over by Birmingham and as part of the deal the City agreed to build on the Moseley Road a library, opened in 1896, and public washing baths and swimming baths, in use from 1907. That same year a depot was opened for electric trams, steam trams having ended their service on New Year's Day 1906. Located on the corner of Trafalgar Road it is a striking building designed to match 'the select residential area' in which it was placed. Further back into town was the School of Art, which was opened in 1900 – across the road from which was the Church of Christ. Now a centre for Islamic Relief it was in use from 1912, as was the local fire station. This was knocked down sixty years later and replaced with the building that is there now.

Closer to Camp Hill was the Friends Institute, which still dominates this end of the Moseley Road. Built in 1899 it was paid for by Richard Cadbury so that the Society of Friends might run Sunday School classes, clubs and meetings. It included a hall that seated 2,000, a café, gym, and 37 classrooms. Other facilities on the Moseley Road included the 'Imperial' picture house that most recently became the Cave Arts Centre and was knocked down in 2006. Then there were the 'Moseley' and the 'Alhambra' cinemas, and the most attractive 'New Inns' public house opened in 1990 and which had a cab stand outside.

Unhappily the Moseley Road, its businesses and its status as a civic centre suffered badly from the imposition of road traffic schemes in the 1980s. A new road called Haden Way was built to take the A435 from just before Saint Paul's Road down to the Belgrave Middleway (where Hick Street used to be). Belgrave Middleway itself ran into the new Highgate Middleway, which destroyed most of Stratford Place but not, thankfully, the historic Stratford House. Traffic going along the Moseley Road was unable to enter or cross the Middleway, instead it had to come back on itself by the Friends Institute. Thus truncated, the remainder of the Moseley Road went on its old route into Bradford Street. The inability of traffic to drive along the full length of the Moseley Road meant that the section from Saint Paul's Road to the Highgate Middleway became almost a backwater and many businesses closed down. Since then one of the few that has gained prominence is the 'Ceol Castle', which has become a leading venue for Irish and other musicians in the city.

As for the name Moseley, in the Domesday Book of 1086 it was recorded as Museleie, whilst in 1221 it was noted as Moselege. It has four possible meanings. A. D. Mills and other place-name experts believe that it derives from 'mus' and 'leah' and signifies the woodland clearing infested with mice. However, Victor Skipp has observed acutely that a mouse clearing could also mean a small clearing and that as late as 1847 one of the smallest fields in Yardley was Mouse Park. This interpretation carries much weight. The third interpretation can almost be dismissed. The spelling of Moselege would seem to indicate the moss or bog clearing, but as Alison Fairn has stated this meaning can be discounted as it comes after the entry for Museleie. Finally, Moseley may be the clearing of a man called Musa. A berewick of Bromsgrove, Moseley later became part of the parish and manor of Kings Norton and joined Birmingham in 1911.

Moundsley Grove, Warstock

This short cul-de-sac off Grendon Road is the last reminder of the Moundsley Yield, one of the five administrative divisions of the manor of Kings Norton. The others were Lee, Rednal, Headley, and Moseley. Meaning the clearing (ley) of Mund it is given as Mundsley in the thirteenth century. For centuries, Moundsley was deep in the countryside and boasted 30 farmers in 1820. It was developed in the inter-war years and after. Moundsley Hall is in Walkers Heath Road.

Muntz Street, Small Heath

Striking our northwards from the Coventry Road in Small Heath, Muntz Street goes over Grange Street just by Green Lane. For people from outside the district Muntz Street is known best as a key road on the Inner Circle 8 Route – and how many of us have wondered as to the meaning of its name as we have been carried on our way by the royal blue and cream liveried corporation buses? In fact, it is called after the Muntz family. Now lords of the manor of Tanworth-in-Arden, in the nineteenth century they were one of the most prominent and influential families in Brum. Originally from Poland, by the late eighteenth century the Muntzs were established as aristocrats in France.

Following the French Revolution of 1789 which broke the powers of the monarchy and nobility, the family was broken up. One of them, Philip Frederic, travelled widely and after a time in Amsterdam he settled in Birmingham, where Matthew Boulton advised him to but a significant share in a firm of merchants. Philip Frederic married Catherine Purden, the daughter of one of the partners, and became active in the business. The couple settled at Selly Hall and their ownership of land in and around Selly Oak is recalled by Muntz Park, given to the local people in 1905.

Their eldest son was born in 1794 in Newhall Street and was baptised George Frederic after the great composer Handel. When he was eighteen his father died and

The Wellington pub on the corner of Muntz Street and Dawson Street in 1959. Notice the 'diamond polisher', window cleaner, on the right.

George became head of the family. He successfully carried on Muntz and Purden and the other family concern of the rolling of copper and other metals in Water Street, off Snow Hill. It was through this venture that he made his fortune. Whether it was his own idea or not, Muntz was responsible for the large-scale manufacturing of a yellow metal which was better than sheet copper at protecting a ship below the water line and was cheaper to produce. Consisting of copper largely alloyed with zinc, this yellow metal was used by ship's builders for sheathing bolts, nails and wire.

Muntz later opened a large works at French Walls in Smethwick, but he was not just interested in making money – he was also a keen politician. A radical Tory, Muntz agreed with Thomas Attwood that currency reform was vital for the wellbeing of Britain. That could only be achieved if there was a reform of the House of Commons, whereby the vote would be given to the middle and working class and industrial towns such as Birmingham would each have their own MP to represent them.

With Attwood and Joshua Scholefield (see Scholefield Street), Muntz founded the Birmingham Political Union for the Protection of Public Rights. This was at the forefront of the democratic movement. Huge meetings with hundreds of thousands of people in attendance were held at Newhall Hill and similar reform unions sprang up throughout the country. The Birmingham Political Union was crucial in the agitation leading to the passing of the Great Reform Act of 1832, which gave Birmingham two MPs and extended the vote to middle class men but not to the working class. Eight years later Muntz was elected to Parliament as one of Birmingham's MPs, holding his seat until his death in 1857.

Muntz was a powerful man in his physique and personality and he relished verbal and physical confrontations. Marked out from his fellows by his long, dark beard, baggy trousers and walking stick, Muntz could abide neither fools nor bullies – although his detractors would have said he could be both. Independent, outspoken and full of contradictions, he often offended the Liberal establishment in Birmingham and was looked down as a coarse, stubborn and self-centred politician. Yet to the working people of Birmingham Muntz was a bluff, manly and steadfast champion. He may have opposed universal suffrage yet in Parliament he voted for the extension of the vote to the working class and he supported the working-class Chartist movement.

However he may have been regarded, the significance of Muntz to the making of Birmingham cannot be denied. Nor can that of his younger brother, Philip Henry, who was Birmingham's second mayor from 1839-41 and who was also MP for the town between 1868 and 1885. George himself lived first at Hockley Abbey, then at Ley Hall in Perry Barr and lastly at Umberslade Hall, Tanworth in Arden, hence **Umberslade Road** in Selly Oak.

As for Muntz Street it was cut out in the mid-1800s on land bought by the Birmingham Freehold Land Society, an organisation dedicated to gaining the vote for working-class men through the ownership of land and the building of houses. All the streets on the Small Heath Estate honoured men like Muntz who had fought for democracy. Dawson Street recalled George Dawson, vice president of the Society and a charismatic and influential preacher. It disappeared in the 1960s and now is playing fields. Wright Street comes from John Skirrow Wright, an ardent reformer and Liberal councillor; Hawkes Street of Henry Hawkes, a Mayor of Birmingham in 1852; and Baker Street from George Baker, another Mayor and a Quaker involved in humanitarian campaigns.

Although never a major shopping thoroughfare like the 'Cov,' Muntz Street also boasted the ground of Small Heath Alliance – later Birmingham City FC. The club moved there from the Ladypool Road, Sparkbrook, in 1877 and remained at the site until St Andrew's was acquired. Today the countryside is far from Muntz Street but its name still calls out the presence of one of the most remarkable of Birmingham's citizens.

Murdock Road, Handsworth

William Murdock was one of the great triumvirate of industrial heroes who helped to thrust Birmingham on to the world stage as a manufacturing town of international repute. The other two were Matthew Boulton and James Watt. Although he never became their partner, Murdock played a crucial role in the development of the steam engine and in powering Britain into industrial supremacy. A Scot like Watt, this supreme engineer and inventor was born in 1754 in Old Cumnock, Ayrshire. He was one of seven children and his father, John was a miller and millwright. His name was then spelled Murdoch but over time it became Murdock. William's mother, Anne, was sister of the agent for the Boswell estates, which the mill served. James Boswell himself visited Boulton and Watt's celebrated Soho works in March 1776, and his tales of that wondrous place may have inspired the young Murdock the next year to head for Birmingham, then one of the most exciting places in the world – a place where the new world was in the making.

Broad and over six feet tall, Murdock was of a practical turn and had a passion for solving mechanical problems. Within months he became Boulton and Watt's principal pattern maker and an assistant engine erector and in less than two years he was erecting an engine on his own. In fact this was only Boulton and Watt's fourth such engine. Thenceforth Murdock made improvements to Watt's design, especially whilst he was responsible for Boulton and Watt's engines in the tin mines of Cornwall. Murdock spent twenty years there from1779 and Boulton and Watt began to realise they had 'the most active man and best engine erector' they had seen.

With an ability to concentrate on a variety of ideas, Murdoch not only solved the difficulties with the working of the steam engines but also he turned his mind to producing a steam engine which could draw carriages. He successfully made a model which ran around his room at Redruth – but he did not pursue his breakthrough. Like Watt he was a shy and modest man and was not pushed by the drive which had motivated Boulton.

It was also in Cornwall that Murdoch began experimenting with lighting gases given off from the burning of coal, peat, wood and other flammable substances. Soon he focused only on trying to illuminate various coals and carried on his investigations with an iron retort and tinned and copper tubes through which the gas was carried after it had been purified by washing it with water. Along the tubes were openings through which the gas could be burned, so as to determine which coal produced the best and most economical light. Within a short time Murdoch had successfully illuminated his house and offices with gas and had devised a portable lantern. This was supplied with gas from a bladder which he placed under his arm like a bagpipe – the gas itself being discharged through the stem of an old tobacco pipe.

Returning to Birmingham in 1798, Murdoch continued his experiments and in his own words 'constructed an apparatus upon a large scale, which during many successive nights was applied to the lighting of their principal building, and various new methods were practiced, of washing and purifying the gas'. A year later, on 30 September, the Soho Works were the first in the land to be lit by gas. Then in 1802, to celebrate the Treaty of Amiens which brought a short truce in the French wars, Murdoch astounded the people of Birmingham by illuminating the front of the Soho Manufactory with gas.

It must have been exhilarating to witness a wonderful new form of power, one which would propel industry and make light that was more brilliant than that given off by oil, candles or rushes? Thousands are said to have flocked to the premises and were awe struck by the spectacle. On the roof of the Soho House shone a magnificent star composed of various different lamps, while the centre window of the dwelling was adorned with a stunning glass transparency of a woman offering a thanksgiving for peace. The factory itself was illuminated with over 2,600 coloured lamps forming GR (George Rex) and the word peace – above which was a star of 'exquisite brilliancy'. The magnificent scene was completed by a transparency representing a dove as the emblem of peace and a beehive decorated with flowers.

There is no doubt that Murdoch was second only to Watt as an inspired inventor and mechanical genius. Yet, his discovery of gas was not exploited commercially by his employers. Perhaps by the dawn of the nineteenth century Boulton and Watt had lost the vigour of their middle age and no longer were forced into new avenues by their desire for improvement and their never ending quest for better things. Gas was to become a major source of power – but its exploitation was to come from outside Soho. Murdoch never resented this fact. He was devoted to his employers and outlived both of them, dying on 15 November 1839. In his obituary in *Aris's Birmingham Gazette* he was described as having 'a strong and muscular frame' to which he 'united great activity and dexterity, and much energy and capacity of exertion.' He was buried at St Mary's Church, Handsworth and alongside his 'loved employers'. He had lived in Sycamore Hill, hence off Queens Head Road. Murdoch's talents and contributions to world history have been little acknowledged. They should be better appreciated.

Renamed Streets

Present Name	Former Name
Hadley Street, Hockley	Albert Street (1897)
Jakeman Road	Raglan Street
Latimer Street, Lee Bank/Attwood Green	Latimer Street South (1893)
Laurel Road, Cotteridge	Stanley Road (1902)
Lawford Street	Railway Terrace (1898)
Lawrence Street, Gosta Green	Lower Lawrence Street (1894)
Lea Road	Sadler Street (pre 1903)
Leach Street	Wellington Street (1887)
Lincoln Street	Norton Street (1898)
Linden Road	Fairfield Road (part of)
Linden Road, Bournville	Stocks Drive
Malins Road, Edgbaston	Grange Road
Mansfield Road, Acocks Green	Pinfold Road (1896)
Marsh Hill, Erdington	Stockland Green Road
and between George Road and the	Copper Mill Road
'Hare and Hounds'	
Medlicott Road, Sparkbrook	School Road (1893)
Moor Lane, Erdington	Braggs Road
Moor End Lane, Erdington	Harbour Tree Road
New Summer Street	New Church Street (1880)

Further Reading

Michael J. Arkinstall and Patrick C. Baird, *Erdington Past and Present* (Birmingham: 1982 edition).

Geoff Bateson, *A History of Castle Vale* (Birmingham: 1998).

A. H. Bevan, Birmingham Street Names (City Surveyors Department, unpublished manuscript no date).

W. B. Bickley and Joseph Hill (introduction and notes) (translated), *Survet of Birmingham in 1553* (Birmingham).

Vivian Bird, *Portrait of Birmingham* (London 1970) .

Vivian Bird, *Streetwise. Street Names in and about Birmingham* (Oldbury: 1991).

J. G. Hammond (publisher), *Birmingham Faces and Places 1888-92. Volumes 1-4* (Birmingham: 1888-92).

Birmingham Library Services, *The Changing Face of Pype Hayes* (Birmingham: 1994).

H. A. Botwood, *A History of Aston Manor Past and Present* (Birmingham: 1889).

John Thackray Bunce, *History of the Corporation of Birmingham with a Sketch of the Early Government of the Town. Vol. I.* (Birmingham: 1878).

Simon Buteux, *Beneath the Bull Ring. The Archaeology of Life and Death in Early Birmingham* (Studley: 2003).

William Fowler Carter (introduced), *The Records of King Edward's School, Birmingham. Vol. 1. The Miscellany Volume* (London: 1924).

Philip B. Chatwin, *A History of Edgbaston* (Birmingham: 1914).

Linda Chew, *Images of Stirchley* (Birmingham: 1995).

Ronald E. Crook, *Kingstanding Past and Present* (Birmingham: 1968).

Kathleen Dayus, *Her People* (London: 1982).

Christopher Dingley, F. H. Henshaw. A Birmingham Landscape painter, *Birmingham Historian*, 5 autumn/winter 1989 (Birmingham).

G. Dowling, B.D. Giles and C. Hayfield, *Selly Oak Past and Present* (Birmingham: 1987).

William Dugdale, *Antiquities of Warwickshire* (1656).

Jerry Dutton and Colin Green, *Castle Bromwich. – 1066 to 1700* (Castle Bromwich: 1999).

English Life Publications, *Aston Hall* (Derby: no date).

Henry John Everson, *Everson's Moseley, King's Heath and Balsall Heath Directory and Year Book* (Birmingham: 1896).

Oliver Fairclough, *The Grand Old Mansion. The Holtes and Their Successors at Aston Hall 1618-1864* (Birmingham: 1984).

Alison Fairn, *A History of Moseley* (Birmingham: 1973).

William Fowler, *A History of Erdington* (Birmingham: 1885).

J. Newton Friend, *Forgotten Aston Manor in Birmingham* (Birmingham: 1965).

F. W. Hackwood, *Handsworth: Old and New* (Birmingham: 1908).

Joseph Hill and Robert K. Dent, *Memorials of The Old Square* (Birmingham: 1897).

Michael Hodgetts, *Midlands Catholic Buildings* (Birmingham: 1990).

George Jacob Holyoake, *Sixty Years of an Agitator's Life* (London: 1906).

F. E. Hopkins, *Cotteridge and its Churches before 1911* (Birmingham: 1986).

William Hutton, *History of Birmingham to the end of 1780* (Birmingham: 1780).

John Morris Jones, *The Manor of Handsworth. An Introduction to its Historical Geography* (Birmingham: 1983 edition).

John Morris Jones, *Manors of North Birmingham* (Birmingham: 1984).

John Morris Jones, *The Swanshurst Quarter* (Birmingham: no date).

J. A. Langford, 'Birmingham Names' in Birmingham and Midland Institute Archaeological Section *Transactions* (Birmingham: 1870).

John Alfred Langford, *A Century of Birmingham Life or a Chronicle of Local Events, from 1741 to 1841. Volumes I and II* (Birmingham: 1868).

John Alfred Langford, *Modern Birmingham and its Institutions. A chronicle of Local Events from 1841 to 1871. Volumes I and II* (Birmingham: 1873-7).

Francis W. Leonard, *The Story of Selly Oak Birmingham* (Birmingham: 1933).

Arthur B. Lock, *The History of King's Norton and Northfield Wards* (Birmingham: no date).

Joseph McKenna, *Birmingham Street Names* (Birmingham: 1986).

Joseph McKenna, *Birmingham Place Names* (Birmingham: 1988).

Bob Marsden, *ABC of Small Heath and Bordesley Green Past and Present* (Birmingham: 1987).

H.W. Mason, *Austin Village Preservation Society* (Birmingham: no date).

Norman Meacham, (put together by Kenneth A. Jones) *A Historical Tour Around Erdington* (Birmingham: 1987).

Rita Morton, *The Building of the Elan Valley Dams* (Birmingham: no date).

Northfield Society, *Recollections of Victorian and Edwardian Northfield* (Birmingham: 1983).

Alma Organ, *Aston During the Nineteenth Century* (Unpublished manuscript: no date).

Ian Piper (compiled), *We Never Slept. The Story of 605 Squadron* (Tamworth: 1996).

Valerie A. Preece, *Duddeston and Vauxhall Gardens* (Birmingham: 1990).

Mary and Walter Reynolds, *Memories of Kings Heath* (Birmingham: 1989).

Anthony N. Rosser, *The Quinton and Round About. A History. Volume 1* (Birmingham: 1998).

L.F. Salzman (editor), *The Victoria History of the County of Warwick. Volume IV. Hemlingford Hundred* (London: 1947).

Walter Showell, *Dictionary of Birmingham* (Oldbury: 1885).

Sketchley and Adams, *The Streets and Inhabitants of Birmingham in 1770* (Birmingham: 1770).

Pearson and Rollason, The Birmingham Directory (1777).

Victor Skipp, *Medieval Yardley* (London: 1970).

Victor Skipp, *A History of Greater Birmingham – down to 1830* (Birmingham: 1980).

Toulmin Smith, Memorials of Old Birmingham. Men and Names (Birmingham: 1864).

William Hawkes Smith (Printed by James Drake), *The Picture of Birmingham* (Birmingham: 1825).

W. B. Stephens (editor), *The Victoria History of the County of Warwick. Volume VII. The City of Birmingham* (London: 1964).

Will Thorne, *My Life's Battles* (London: 1925).

William West, *The History, Topography and Directory of Warwickshire* (Birmingham: 1830).

Francis White, *History, Gazeteer and Directory of Warwickshire* (Sheffield: 1850).

Frances Wilmot, *The History off Harborne Hall* (Birmingham: 1991).

Donald Wright, *Bygone Bartley Green* (Birmingham: about 1977) .

Donald Wright, *An Account of Harborne from Earliest Times to 1891* (Birmingham: 1981).

R. Wrightson, *Wrightson's New Triennial Directory* (Birmingham: 1818).

Maps

John Bartholomew, *Bartholomew's New and Revised Plan of Greater Birmingham* (about 1904).
John Bartholomew, *Bartholomew's Pocket Atlas and Guide to Birmingham* (1954).
Samuel Bradford, *A Plan of Birmingham Surveyed in 1750* (1751).
Bradshaw, *Plan of Birmingham* (1840).
J. W. Brown, *Street Map of the Manor of Aston* (1883).
Ebenezer Robins, *Plan of Birmingham* (1820).
W. Augustus Davies, *Map of the District of Aston Manor* (1894).
James Drake, *Plan of Birmingham* (1832).
James Drake, *Map of Birmingham Divided into Wards* (1835).
W. Fowler, *Aston Manor in 1833* (1835).
J. A. Guest, *Plan of Birmingham 1834* (1837).
Kelly, *Kelly's Directory Map of Birmingham* (1896).
J. Kempson, *To the Commissioners of the Street Acts, this map of Birmingham shewing the boundaries as perambulated by them in 1810* (1811).
J. Kempson, *Town of Birmingham* (about 1818).
King's Norton Joint Committee, *Map* (1894).
T. Hanson, *Plan of Birmingham* (1778).
T. Hanson, *Plan of Birmingham* (1781).
Ordnance Survey Office, *Edition of 1914* (scale of 1 to 2,500).
Ordnance Survey Office, *Edition of 1916* (scale of 1 to 2,500).
J. Pigott Smith, *Map of Birmingham engraved from a minute trogonometrical survey made in 1824 and 1825* (1828).
J. Pigott Smith, *Street Map of the Borough of Birmingham* (1855).
C. Pye, *Plan of Birmingham Survey'd in 1795* (1795).
Society for the Diffusion of Useful Knowledge, *Birmingham* (1839).
William S. Till, *Street map of the Borough of Birmingham* (1884).
J. Tomlinson, *Plan of Aston Manor* (1758).
J. Tomlinson, *Plan of Duddeston and Nechells Manors* (1758).
J. Tomlinson, *A Map of Little Bromwich Manor* (1759).
J. Tomlinson, *A Map of Bordesley Manor* (1760).
J. Tomlinson, *A Map of Saltley Manor* (1760).
W. Westley, *The Plan of Birmingham Survey'd in 1731* (1731).

Letters

All letters are in the BirminghamLives Archive, www.BirminghamLives.co.uk.

Index